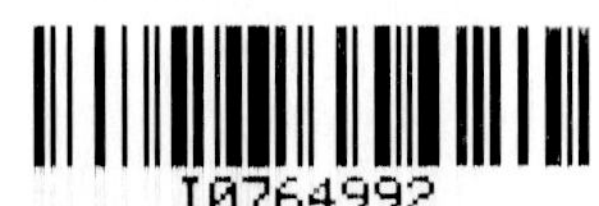

Amazing
COW
COLORING BOOK

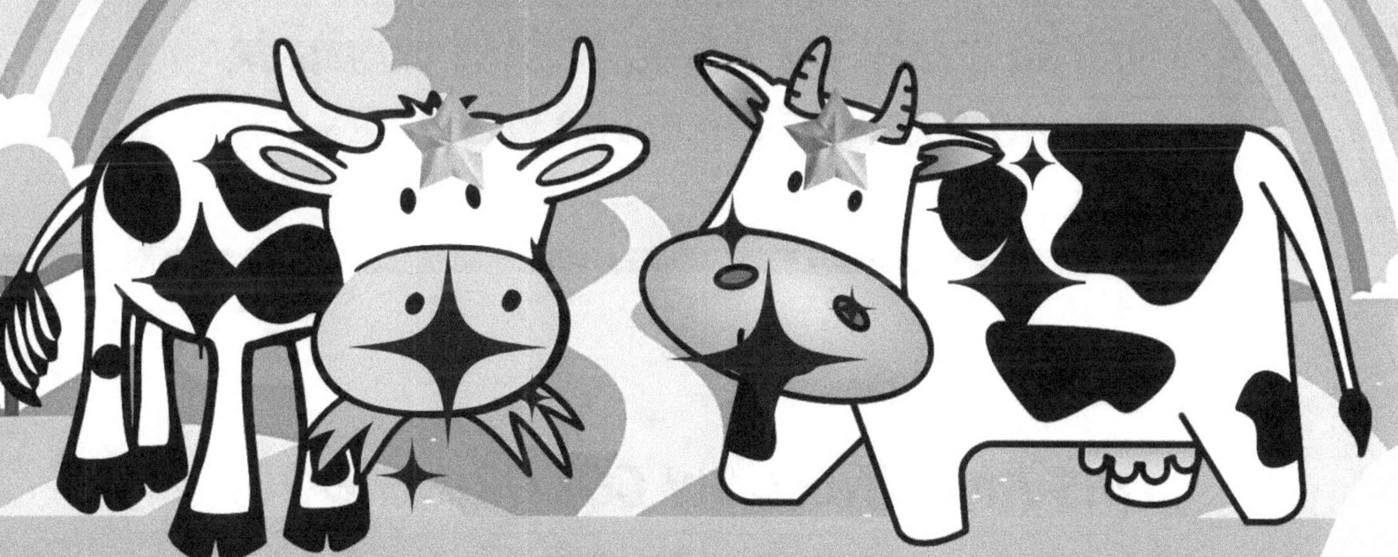

FOR KIDS

AMAZING
COW
COLORING BOOK
FOR KIDS

THIS AMAZING COW COLORING BOOK BELONGS TO:

....

....

HAPPY
COLORING

allrounder Press House

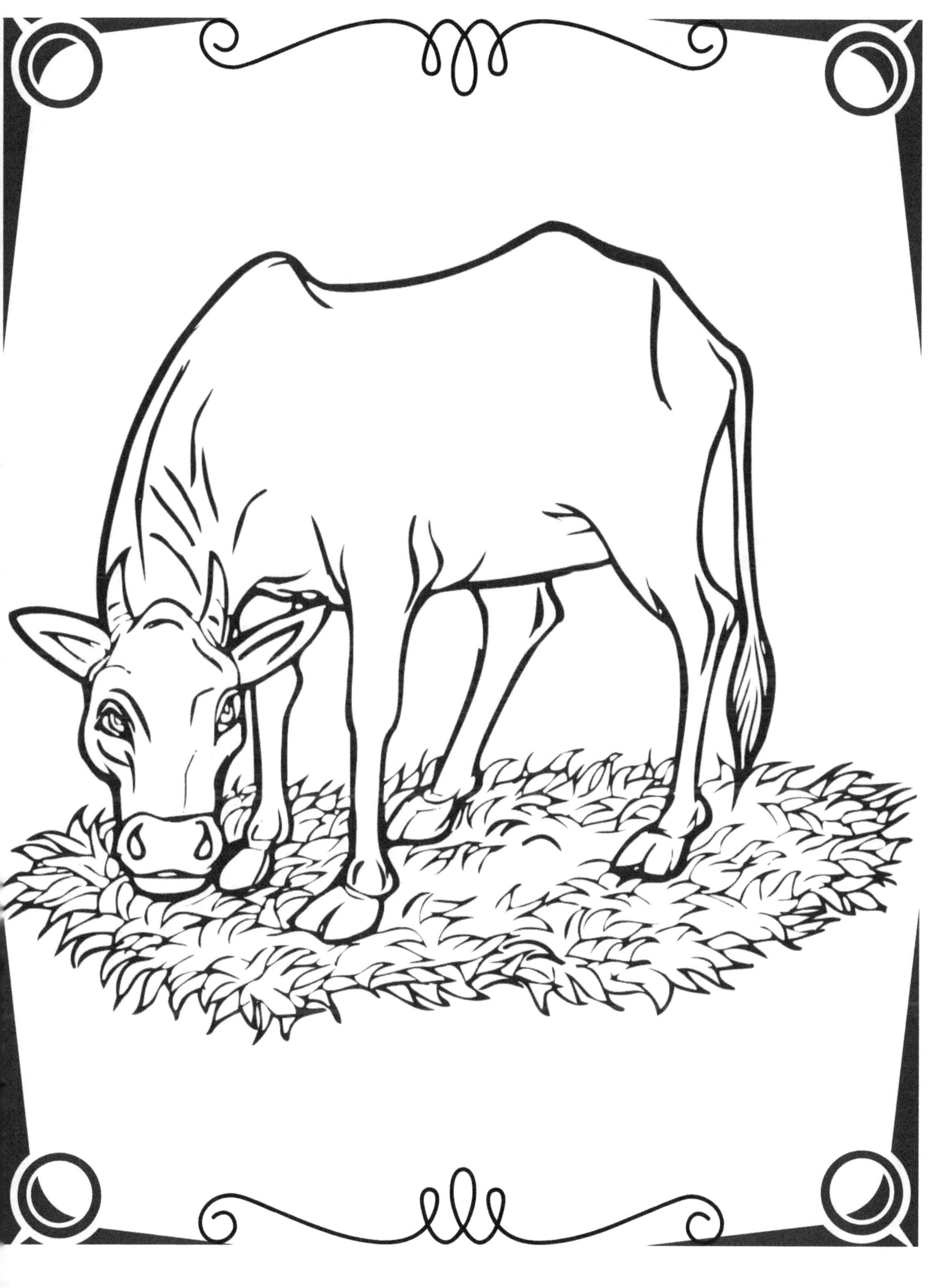

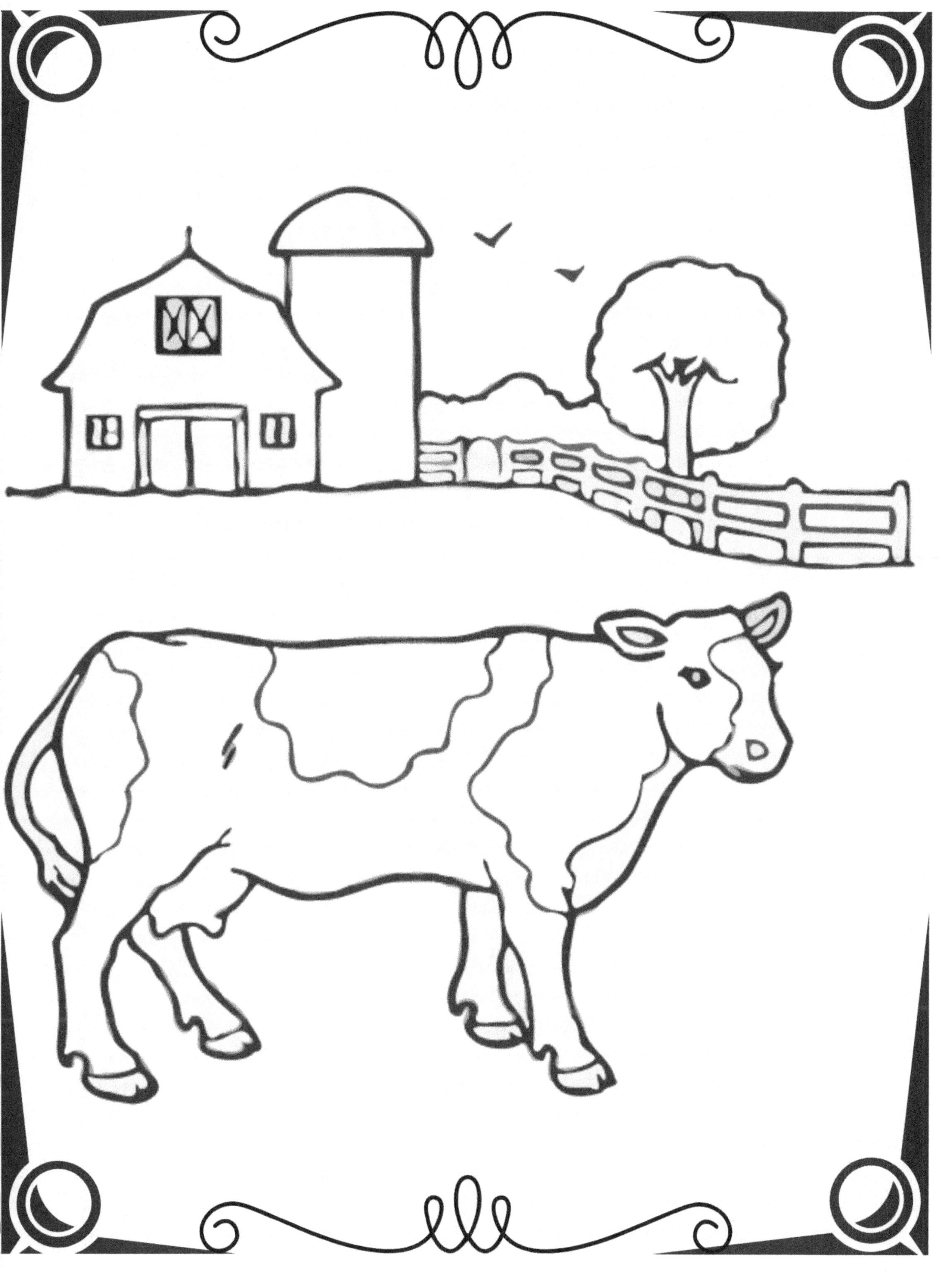

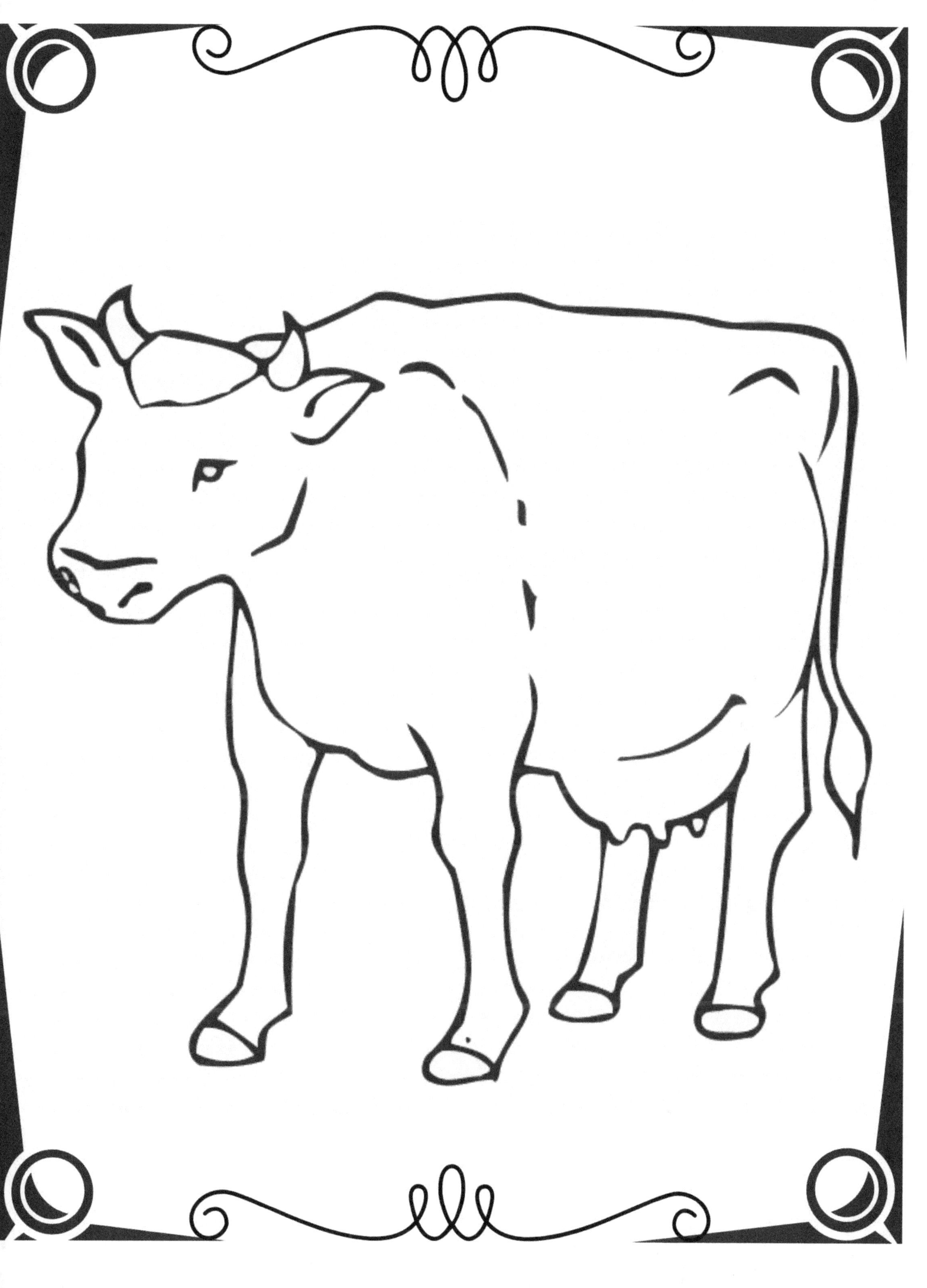

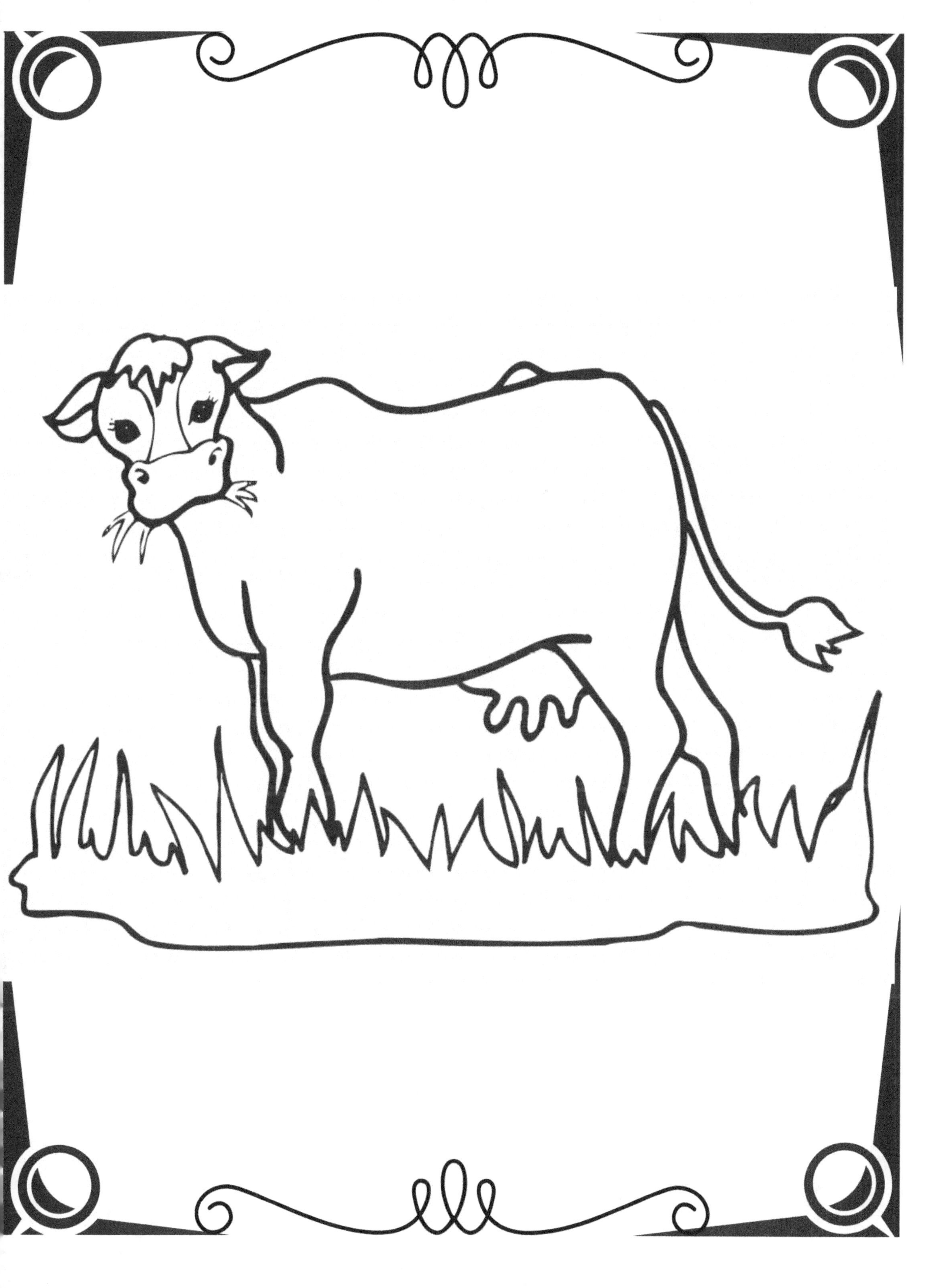

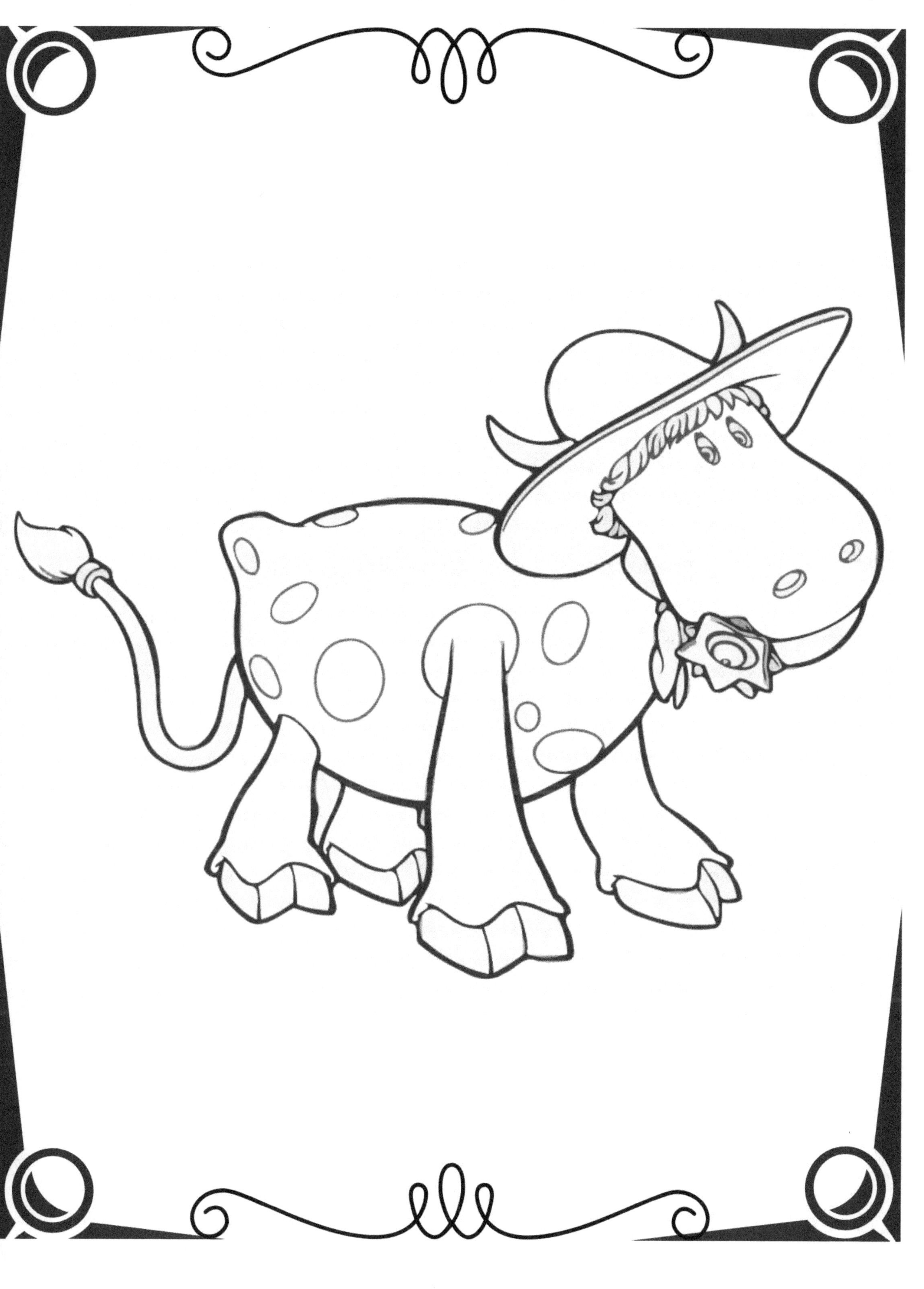

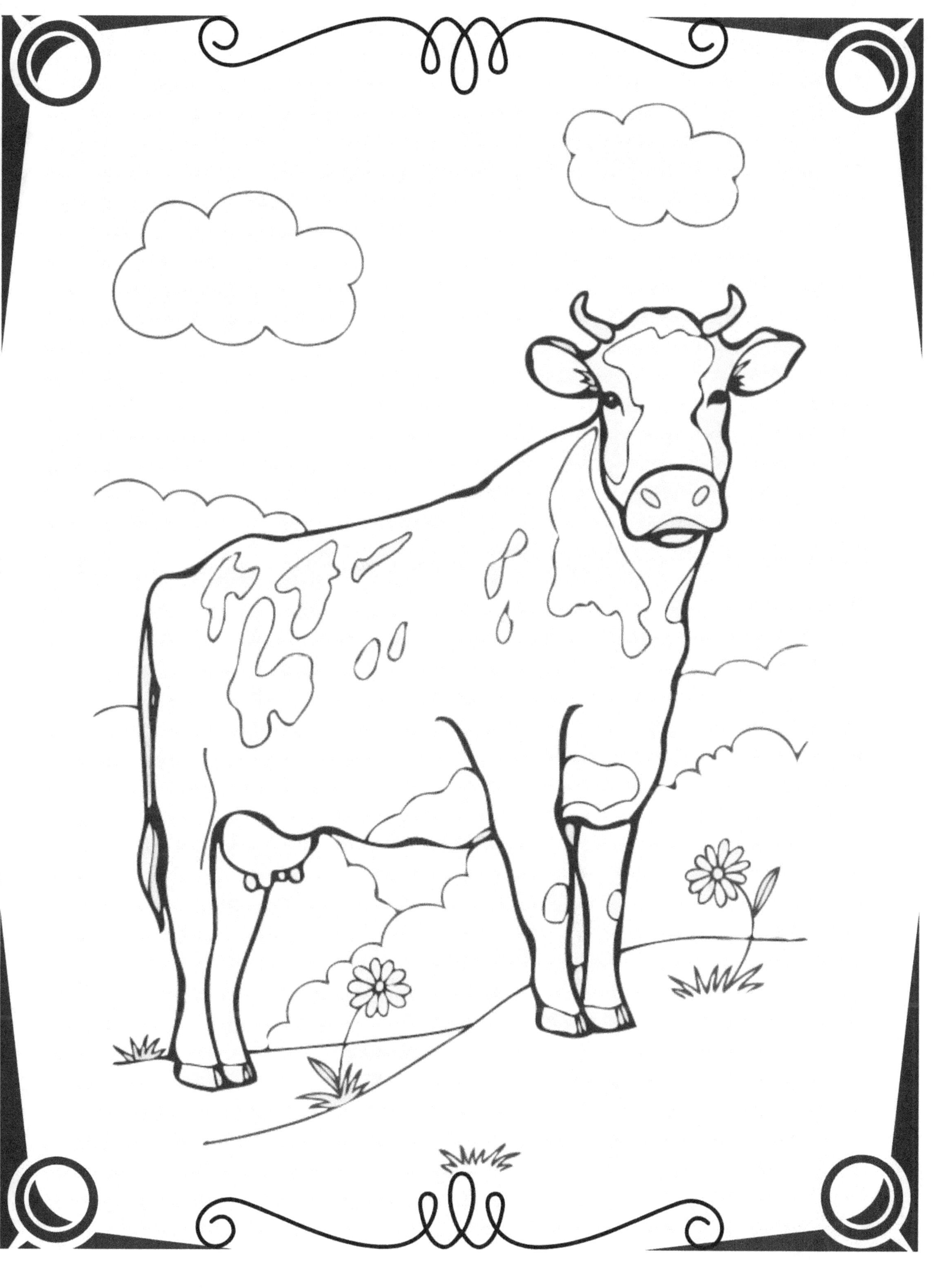

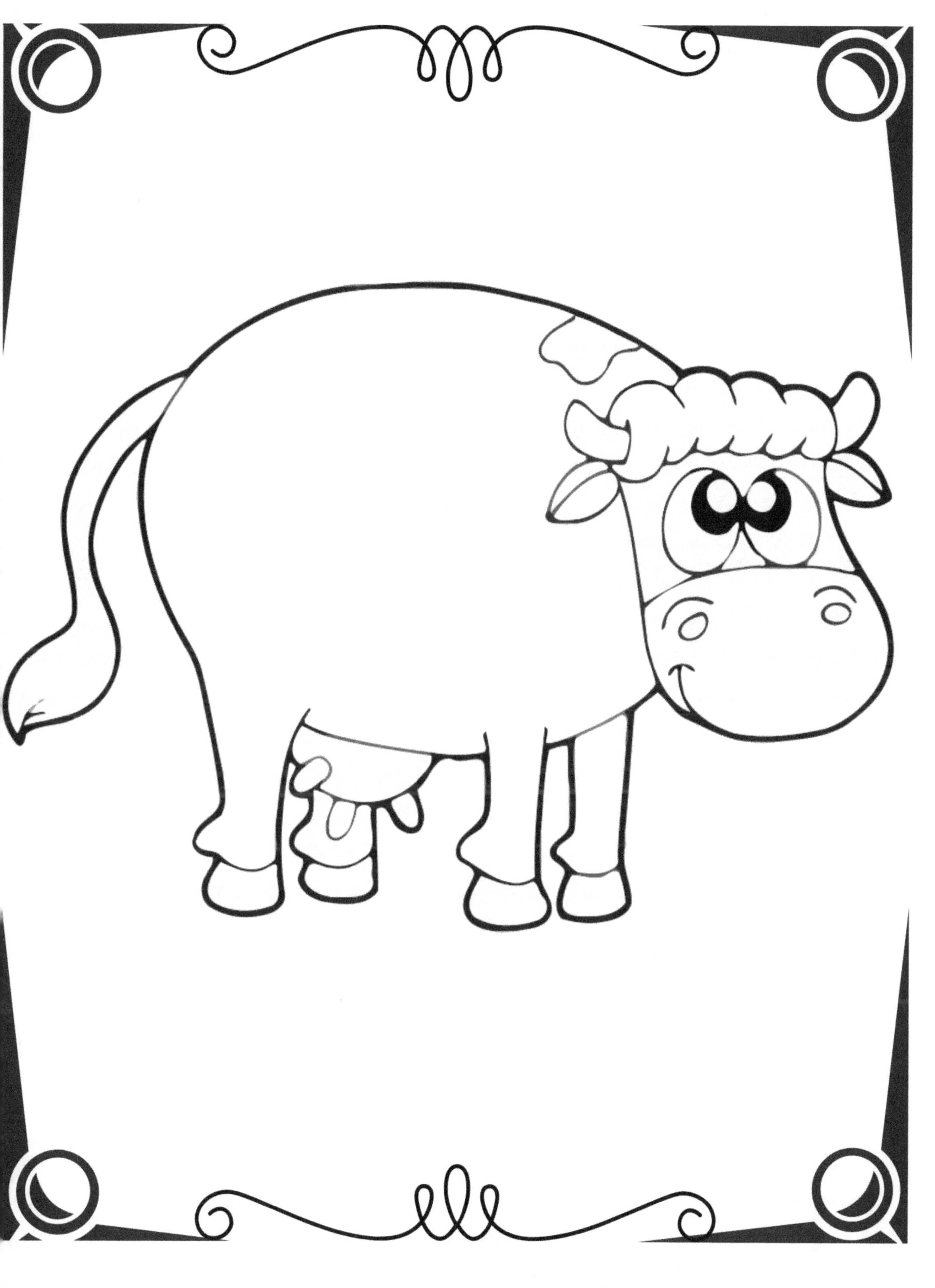

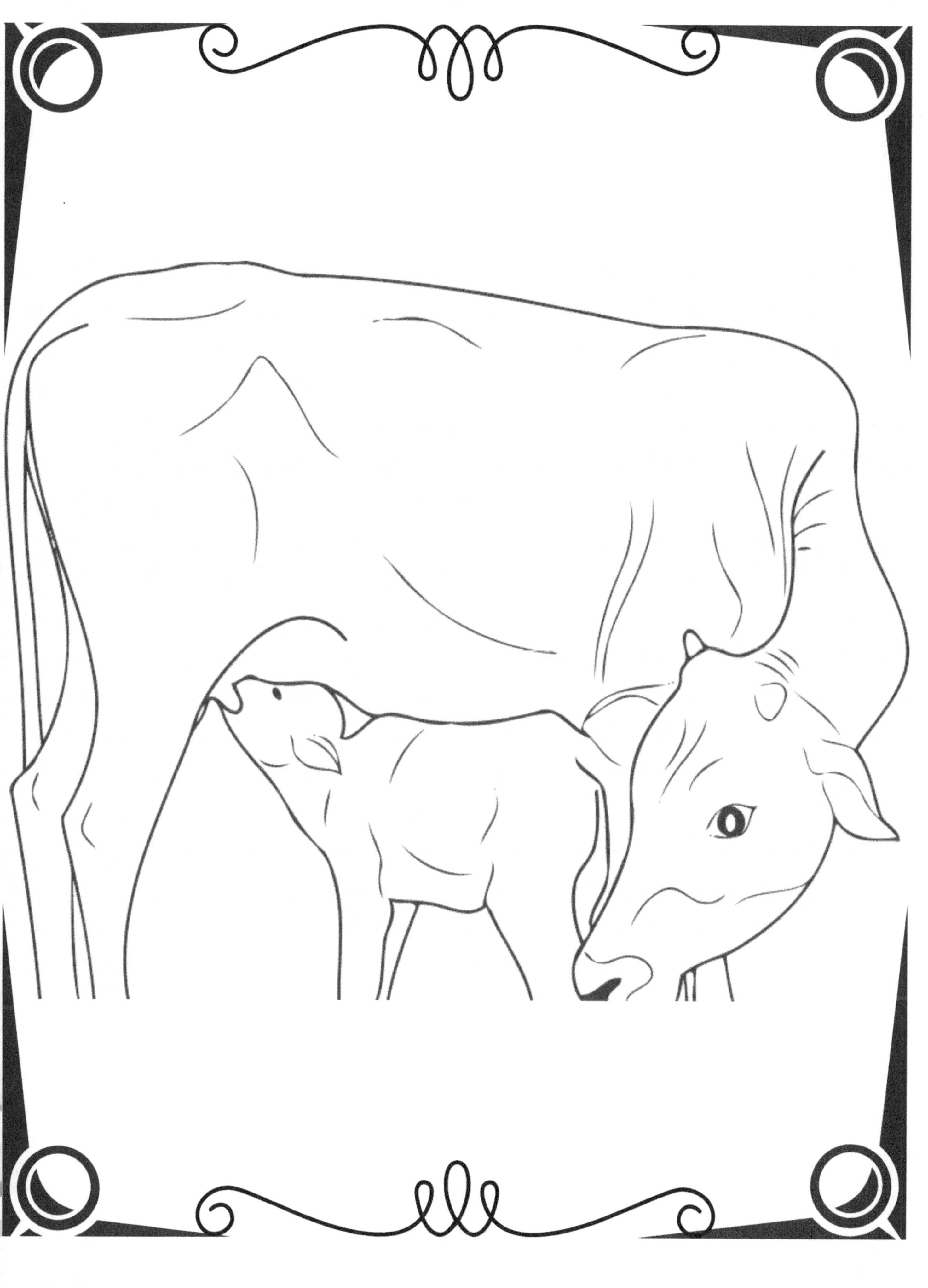

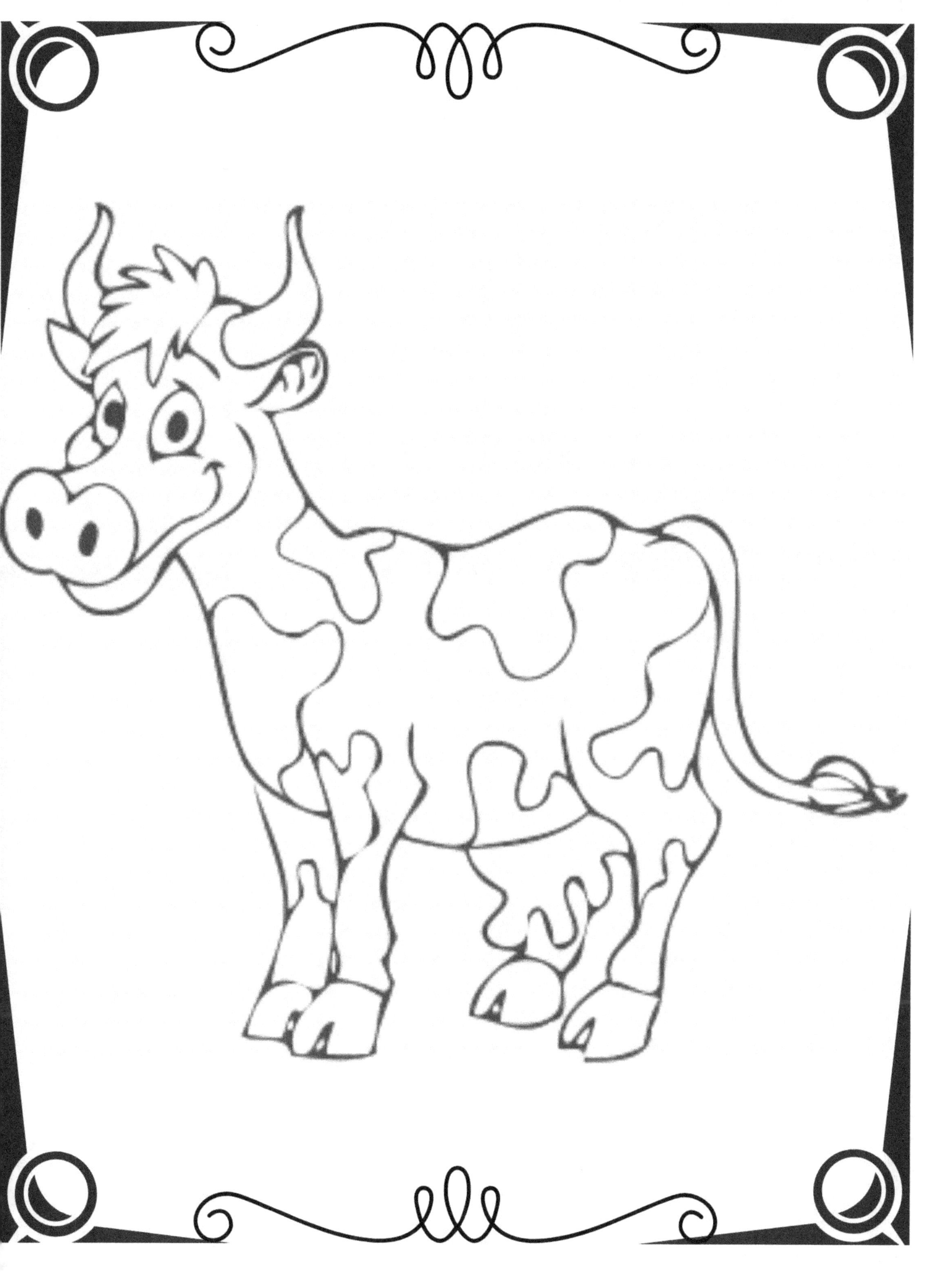

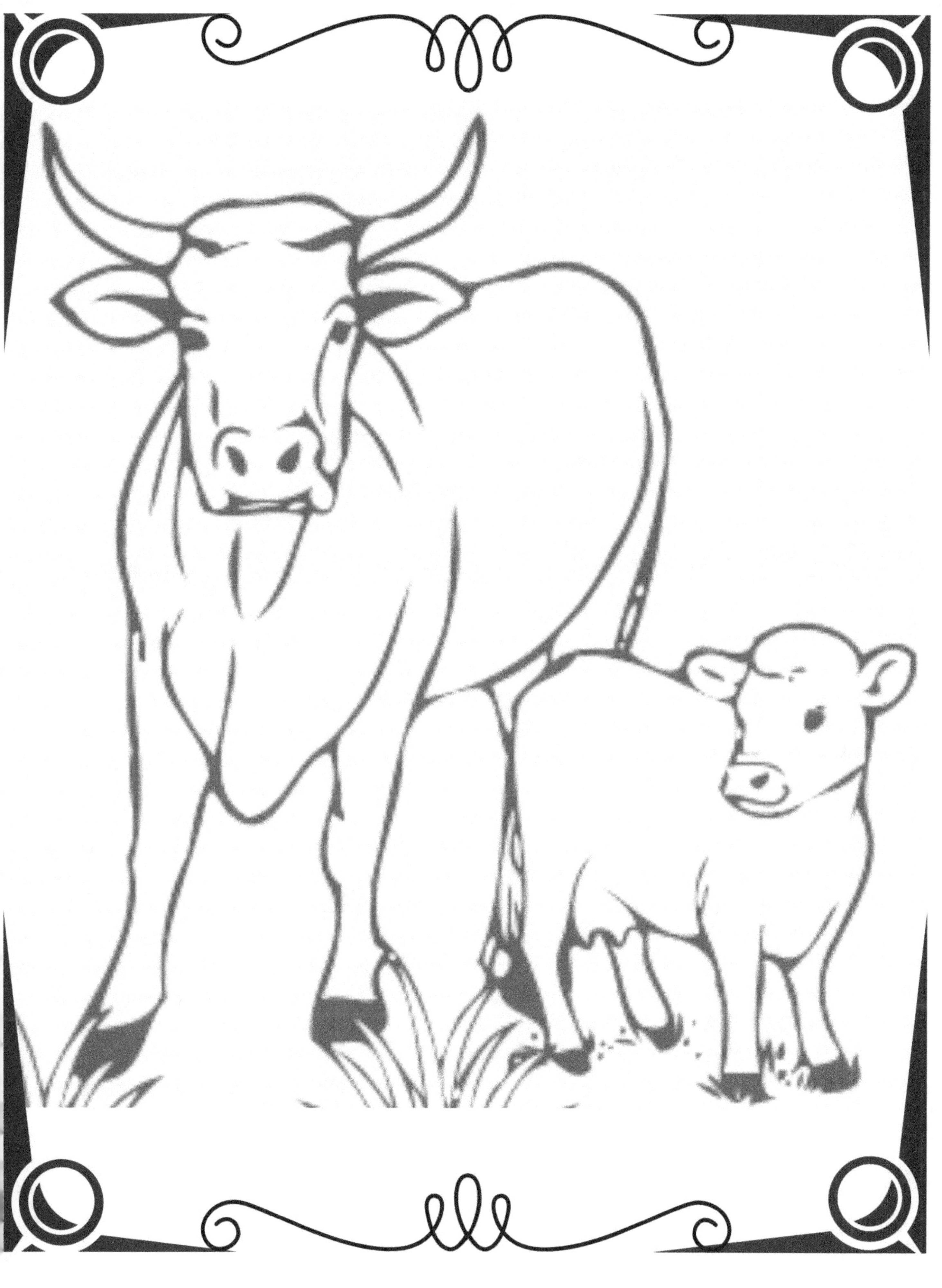

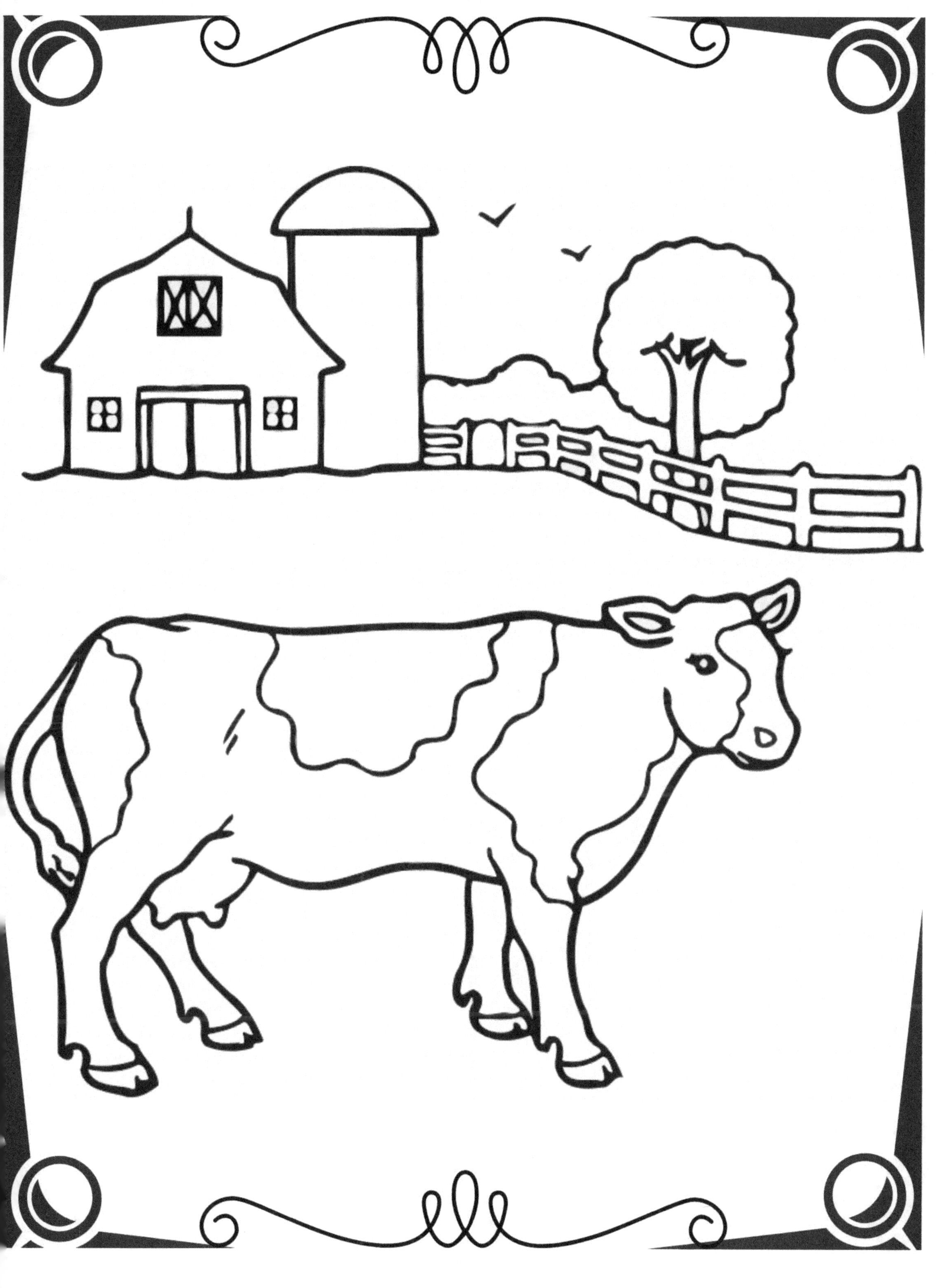

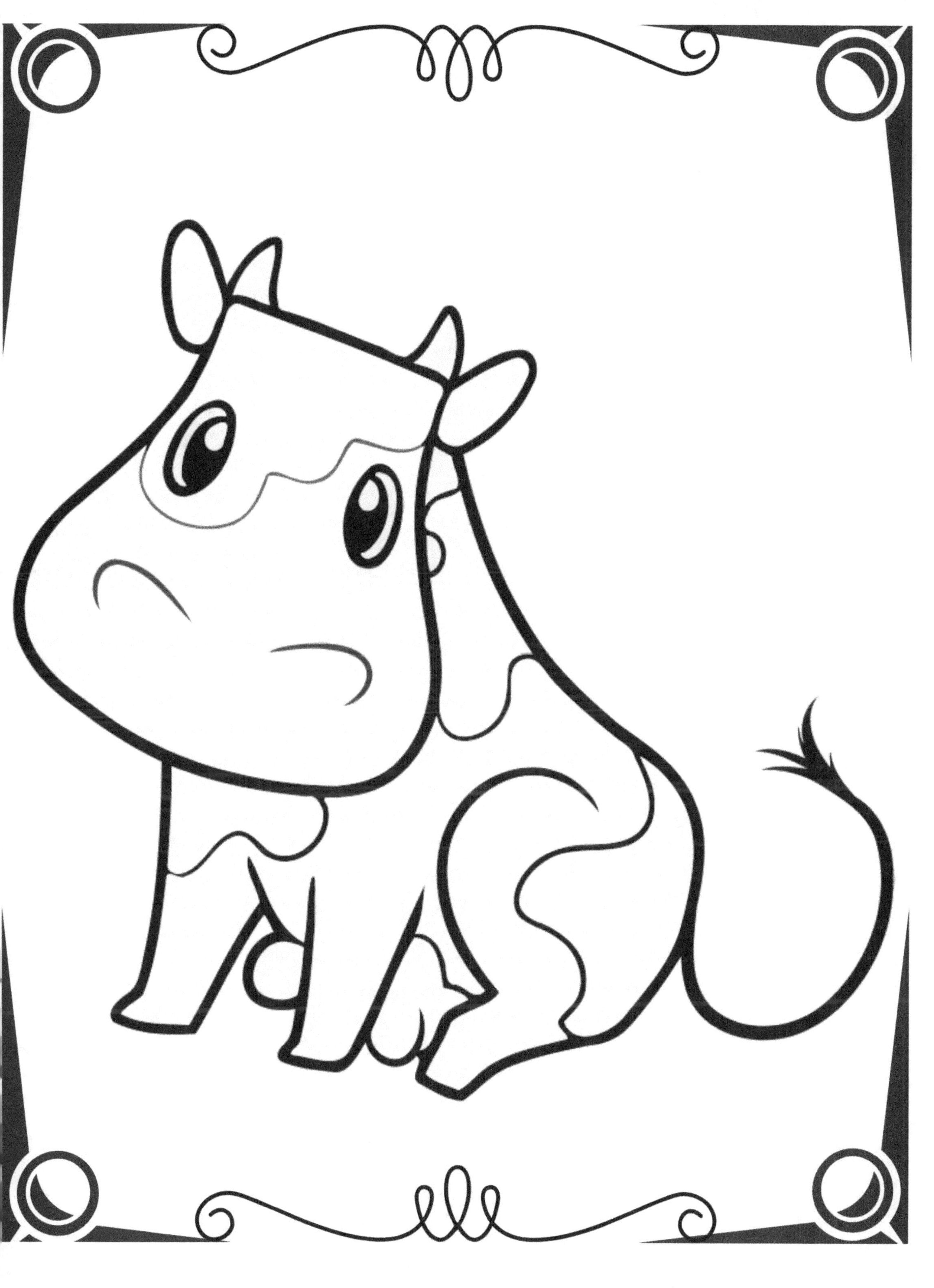

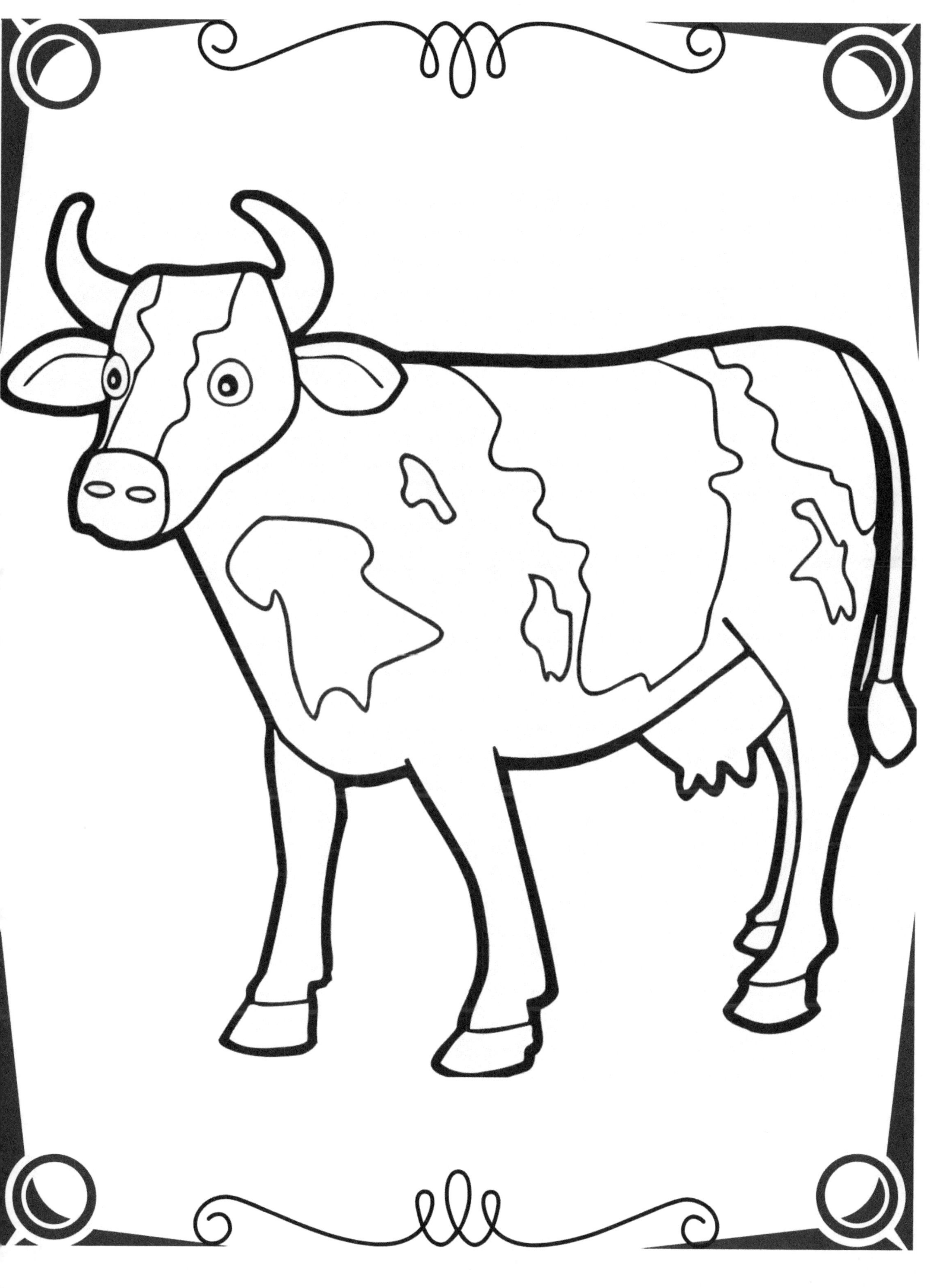

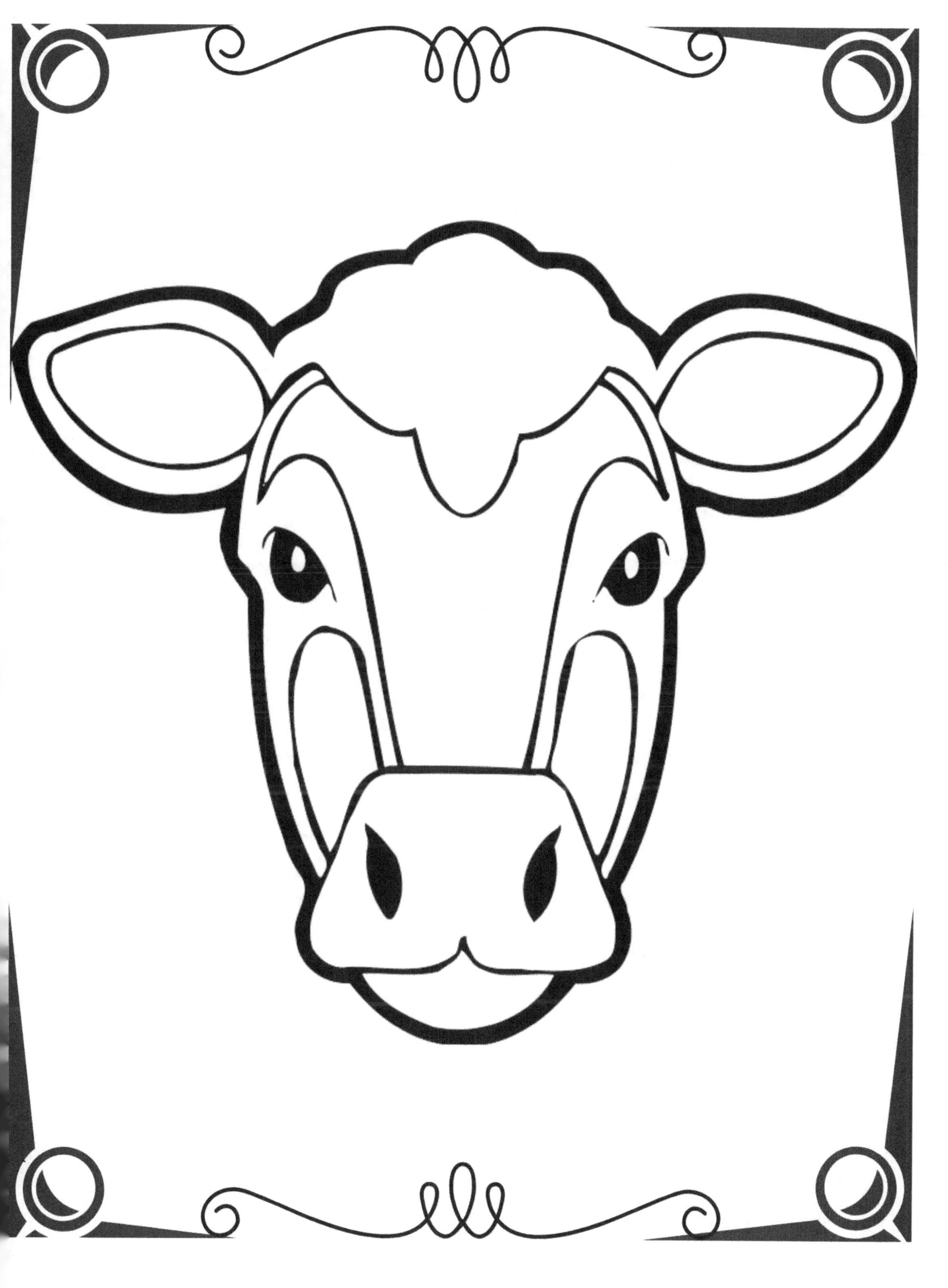

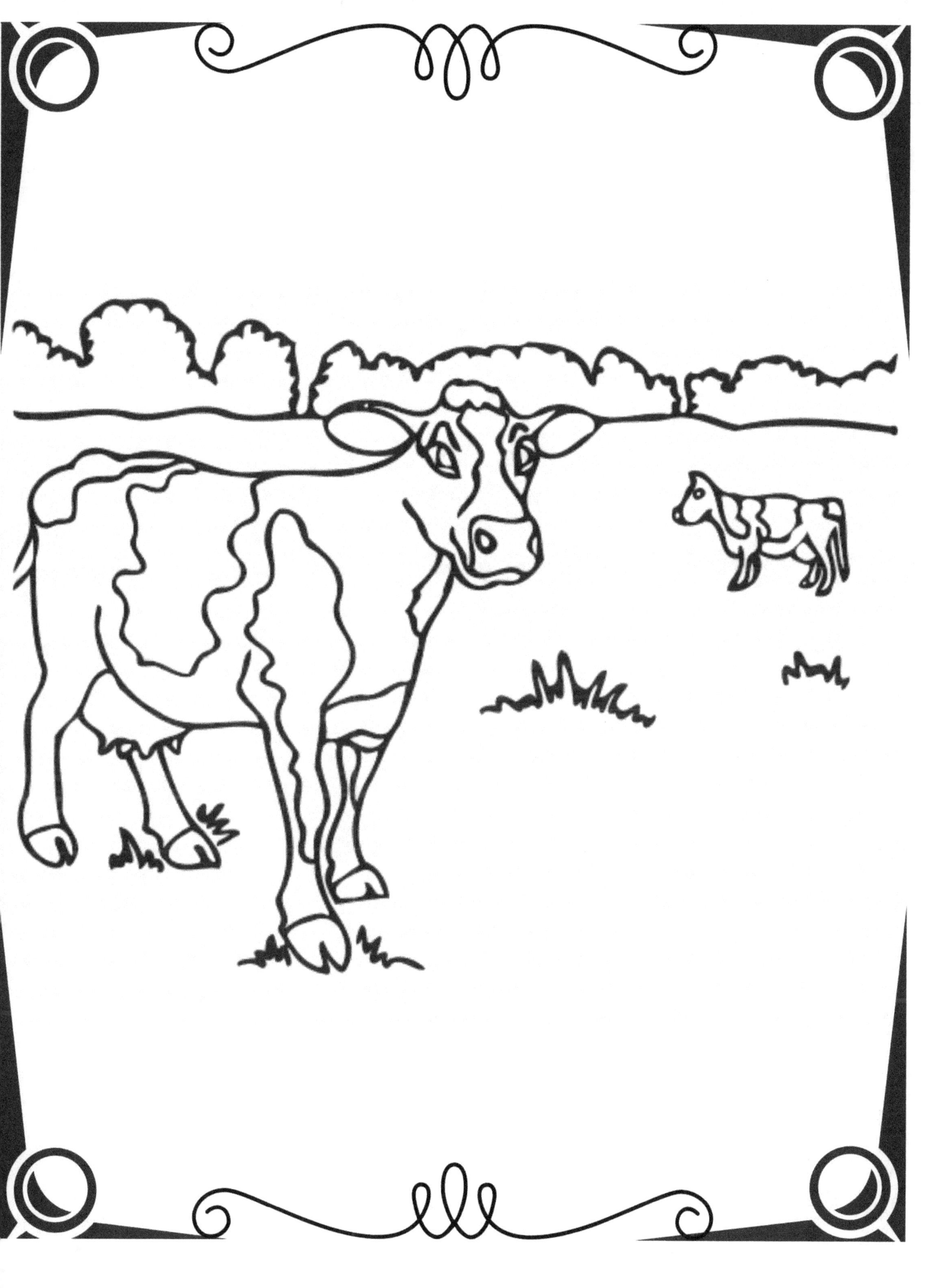

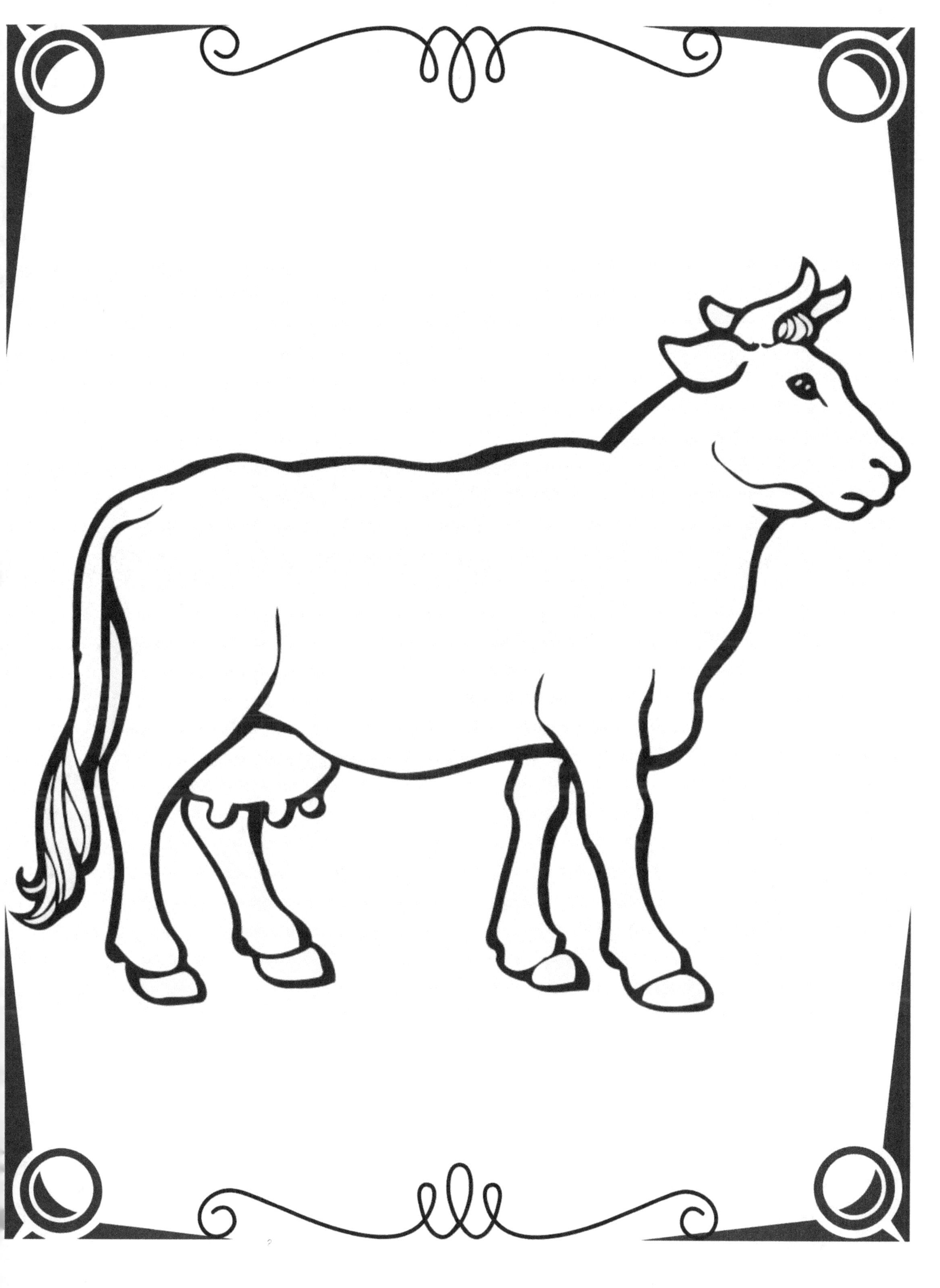

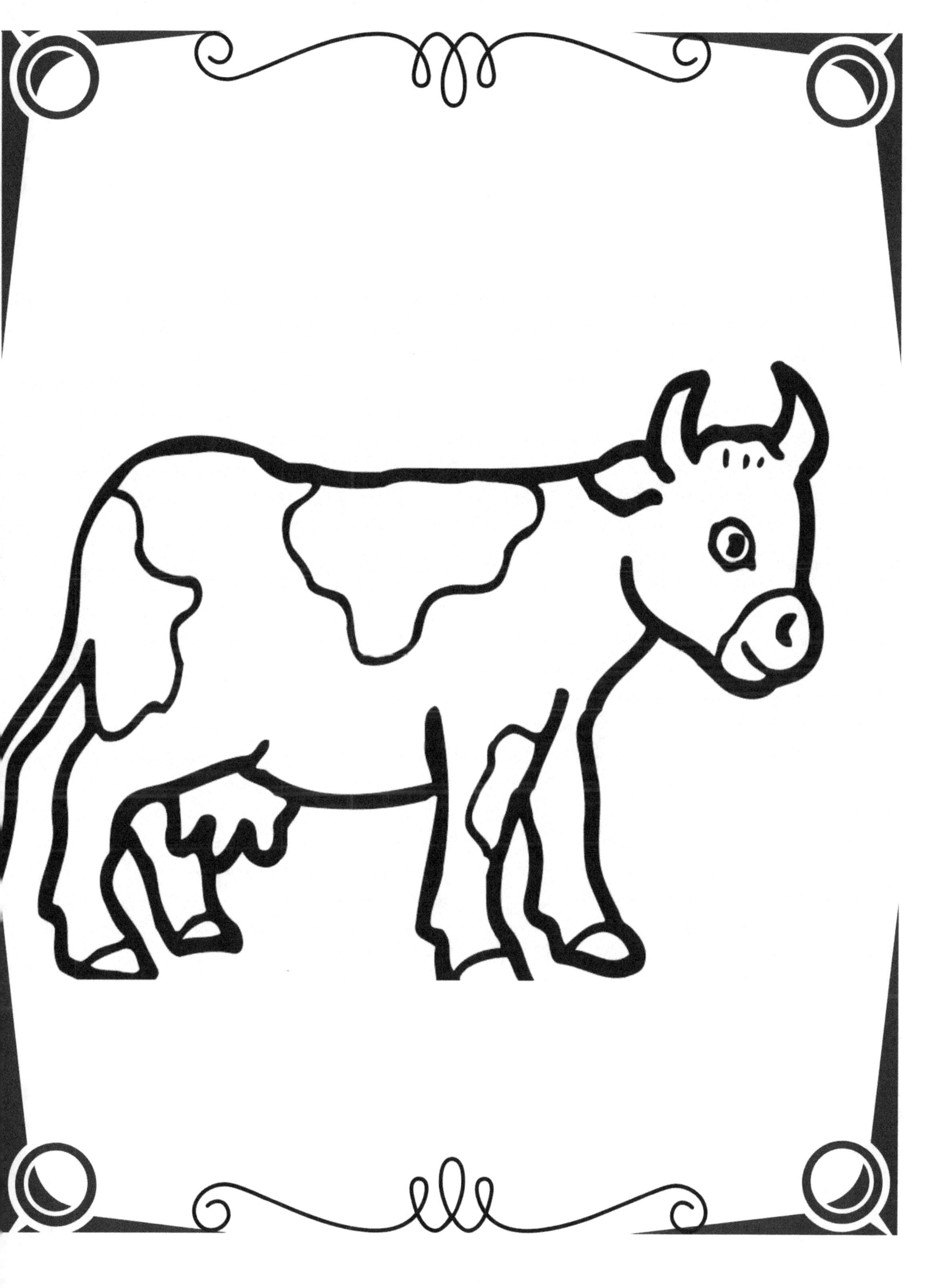

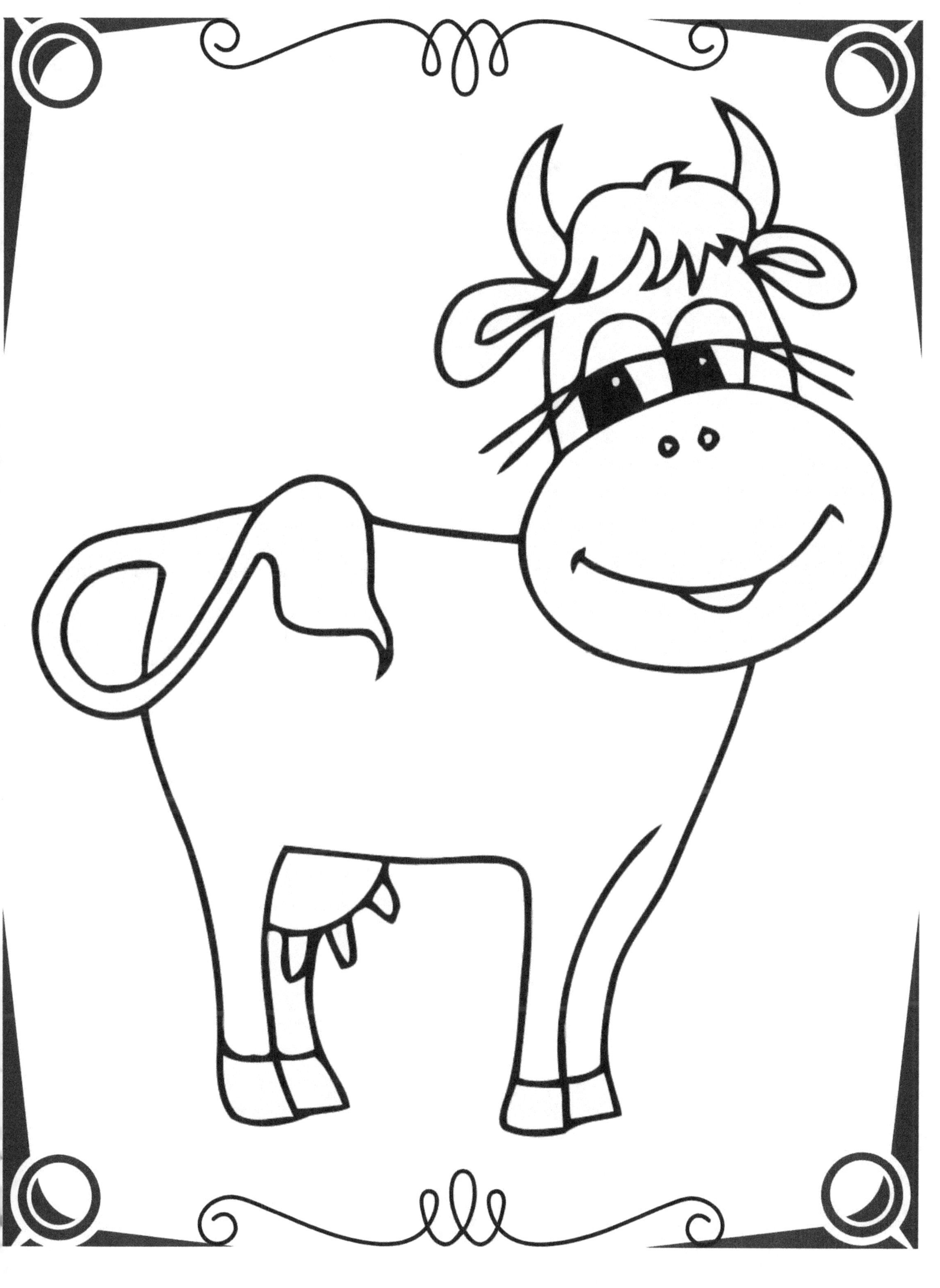

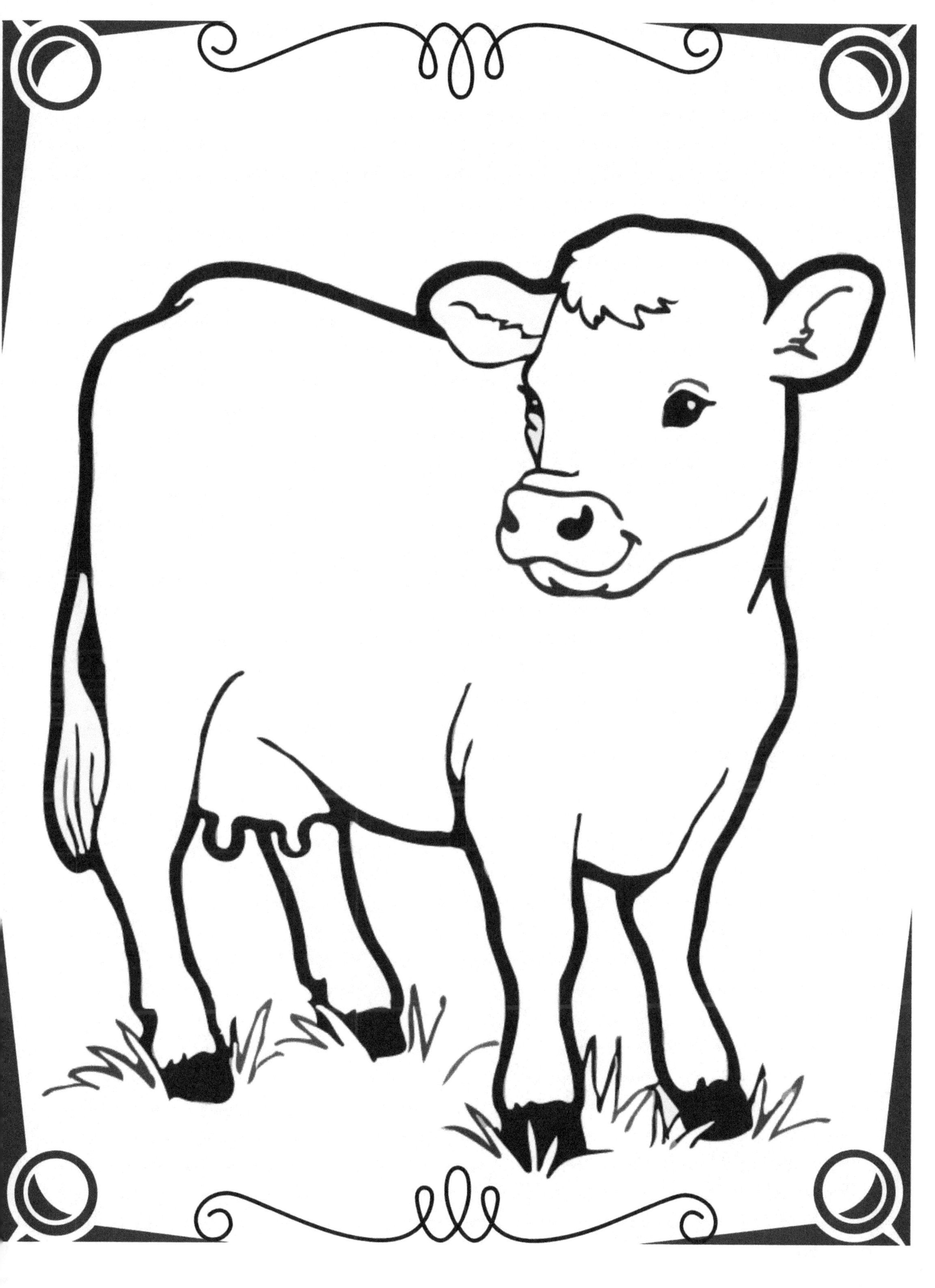

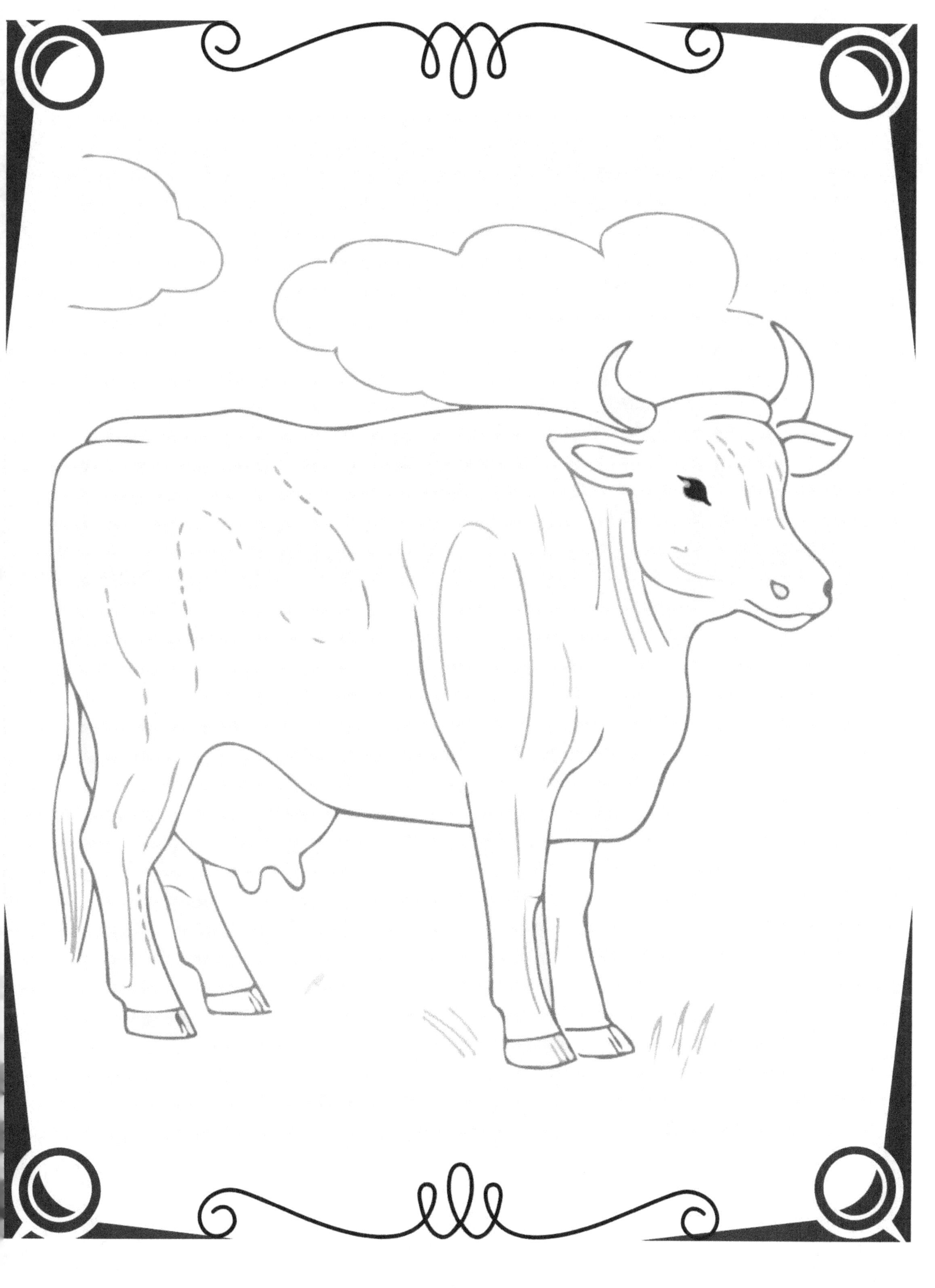

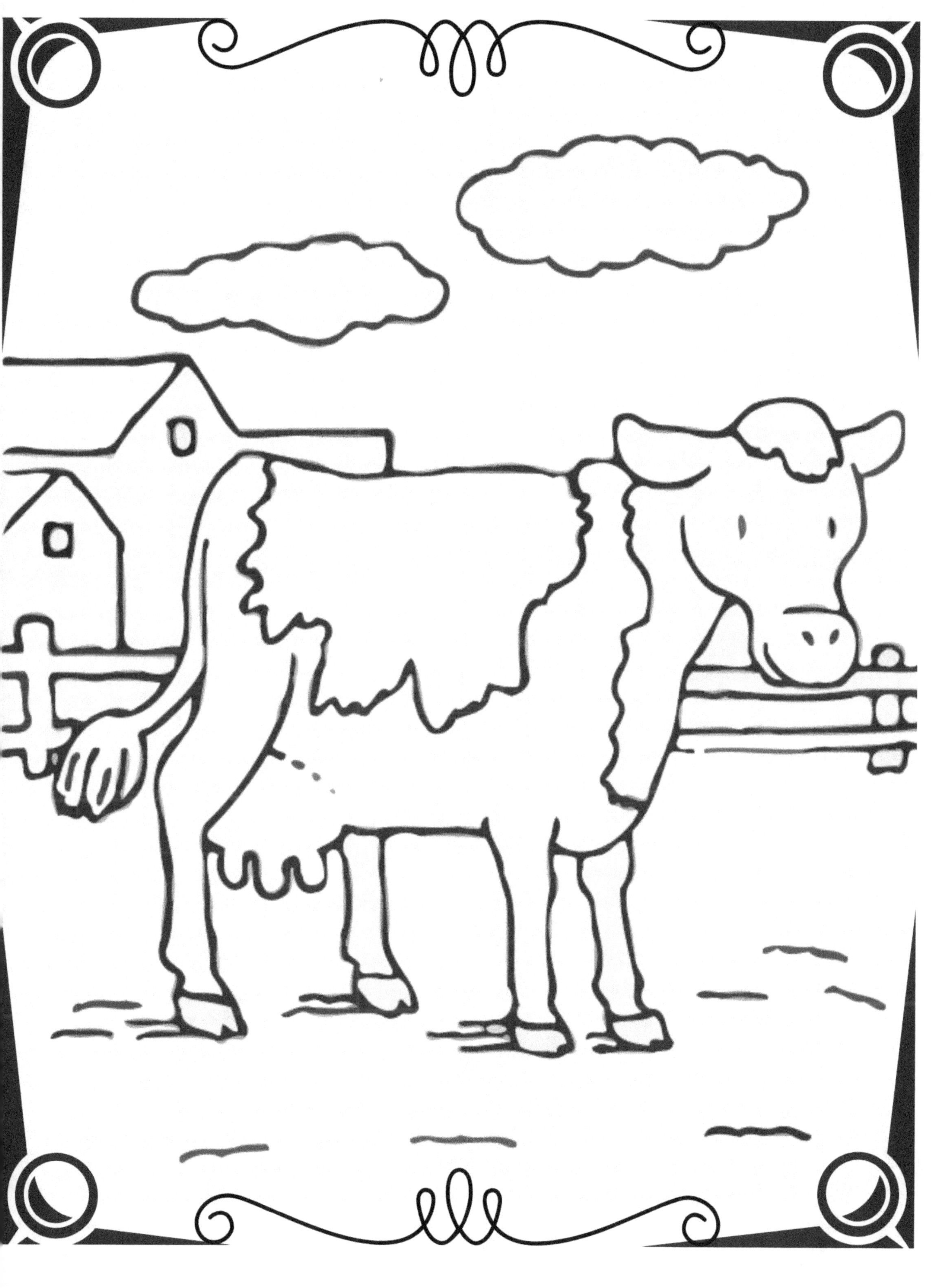

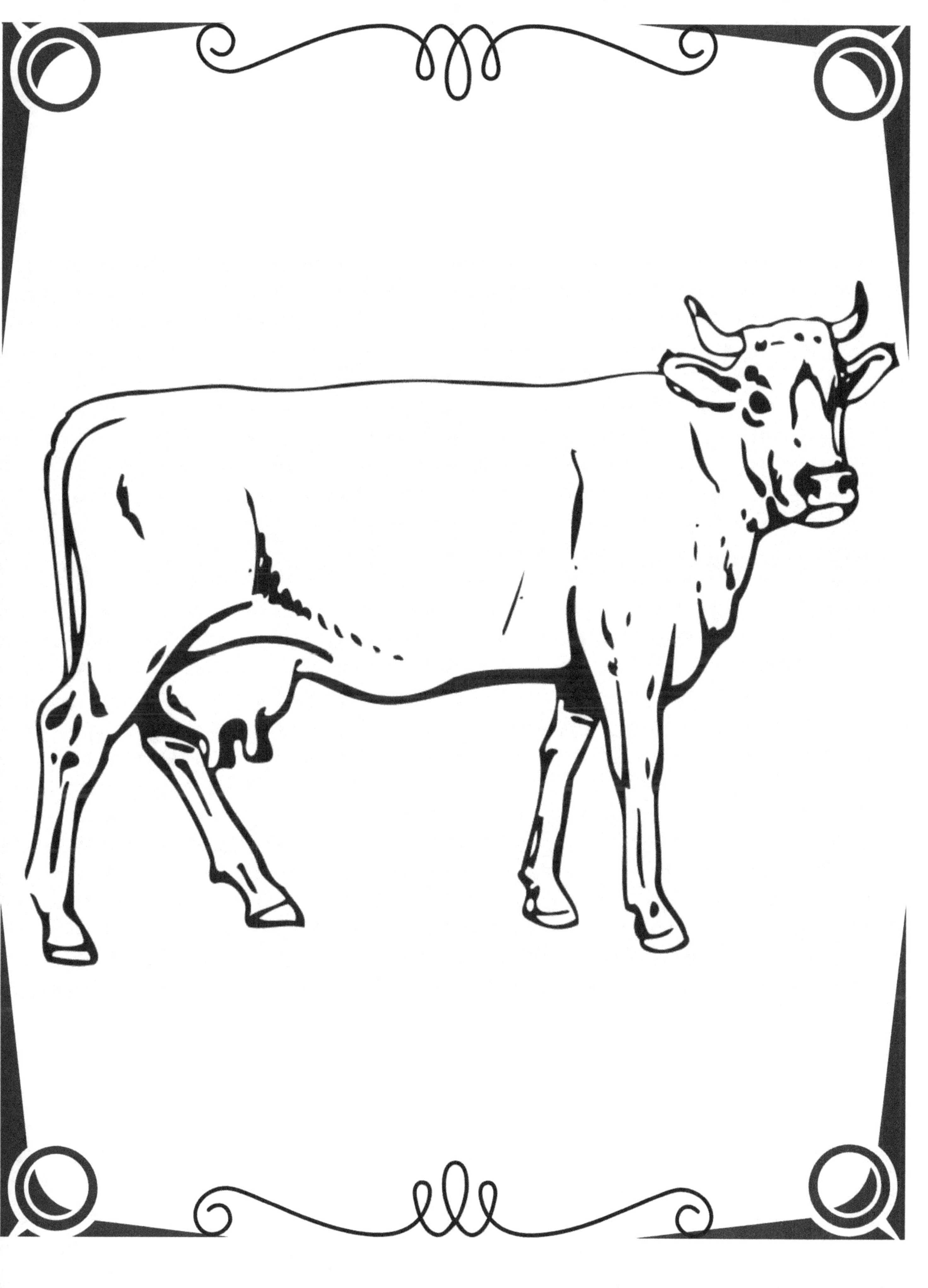

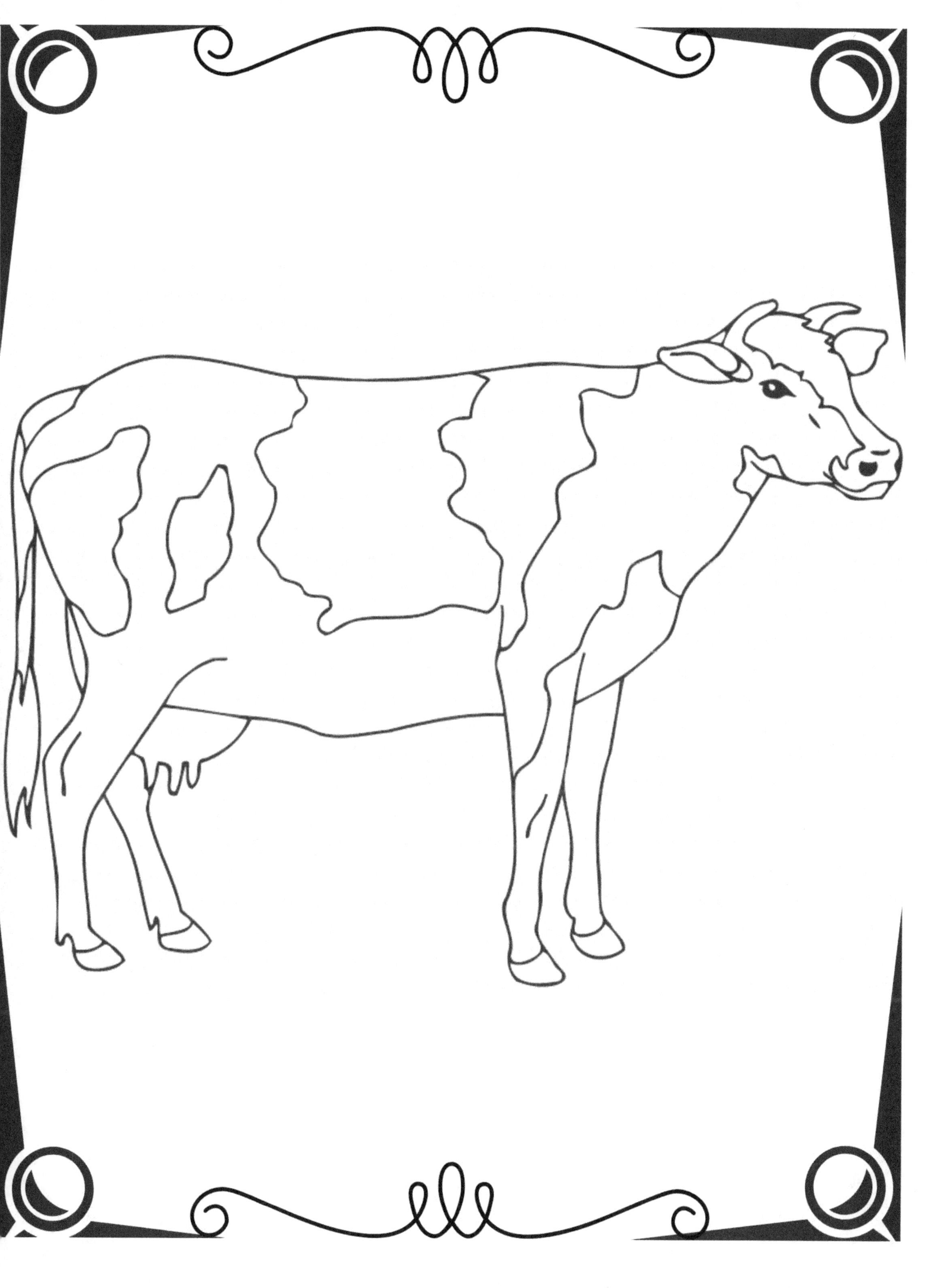

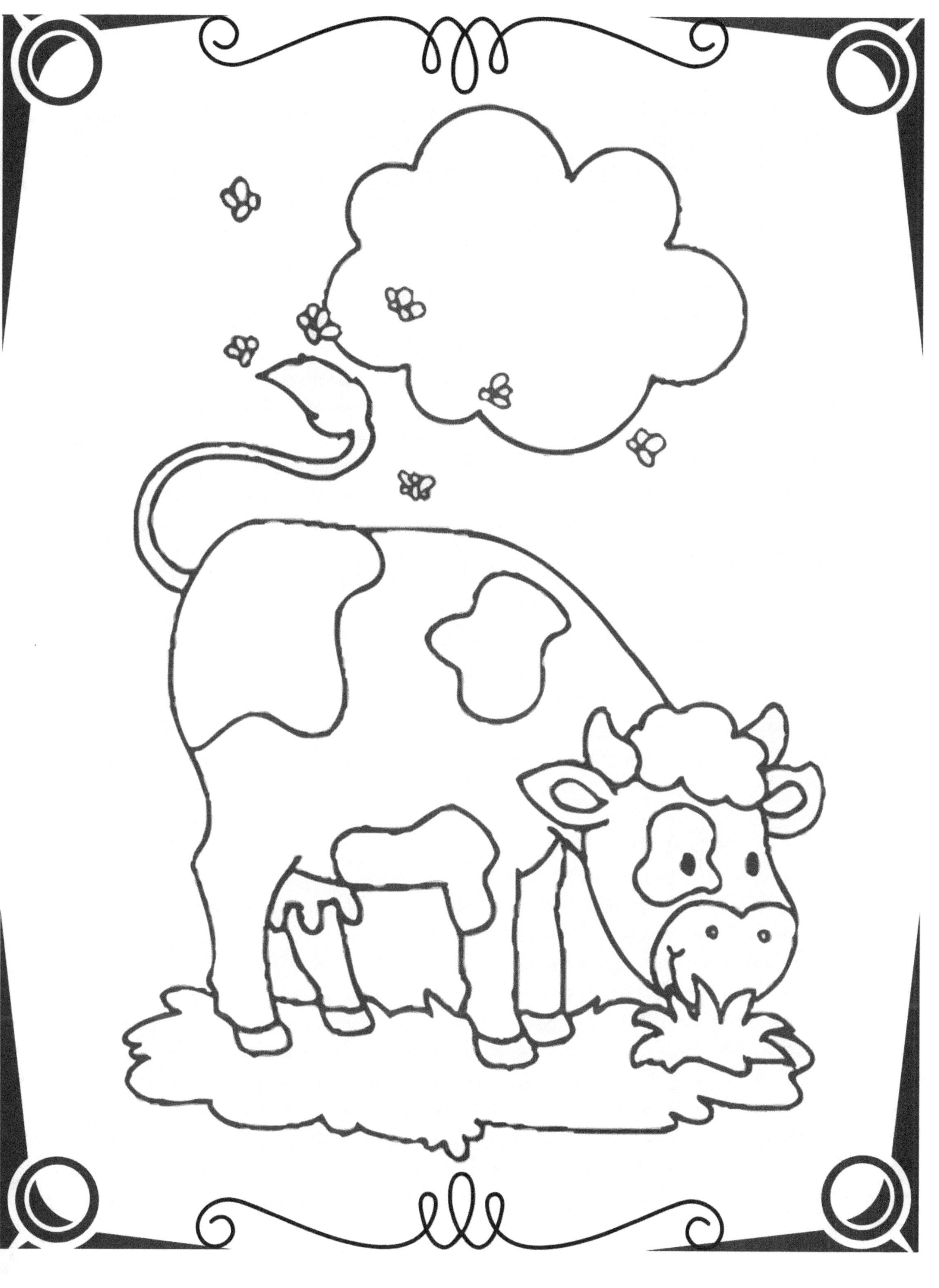

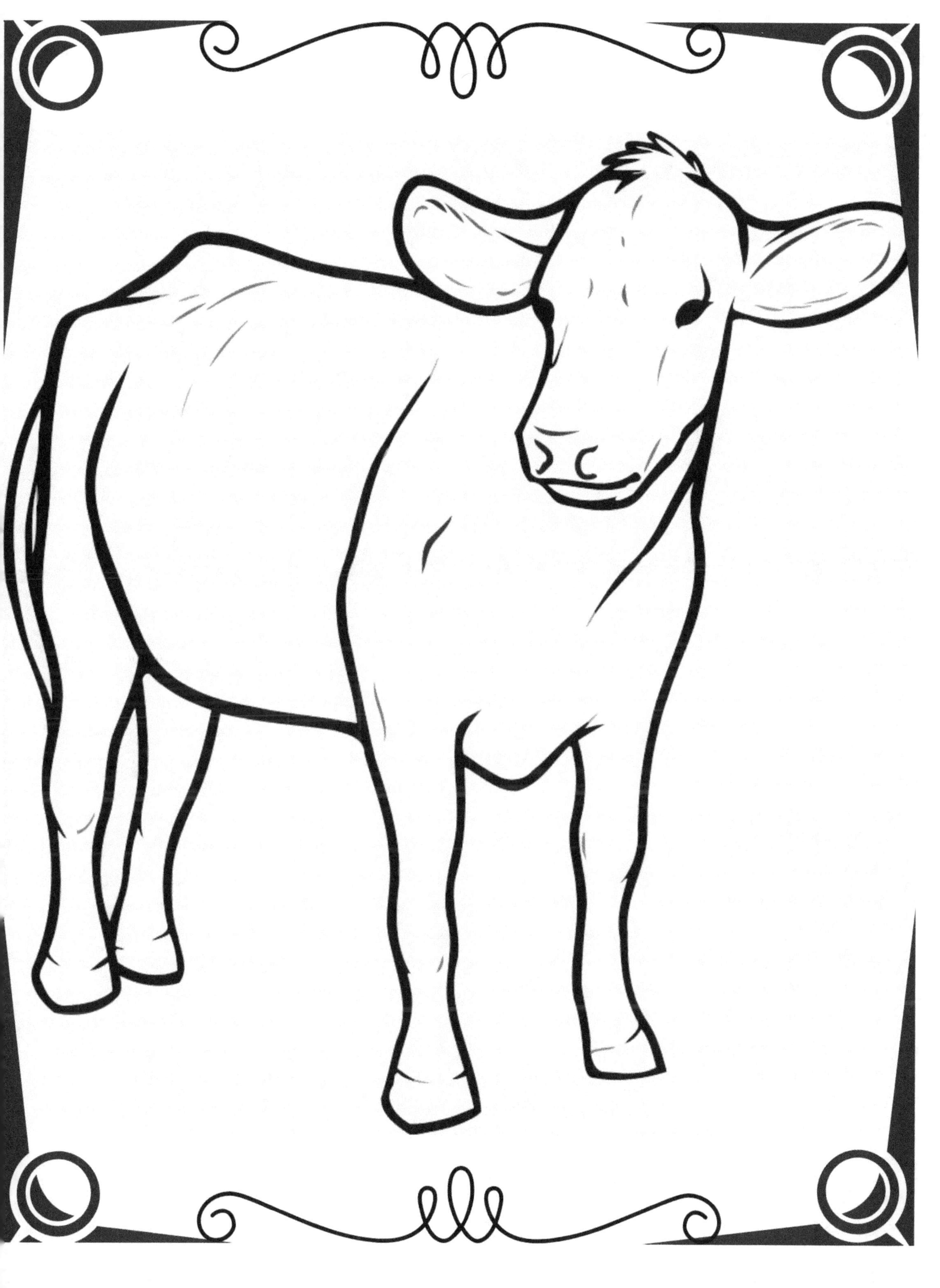

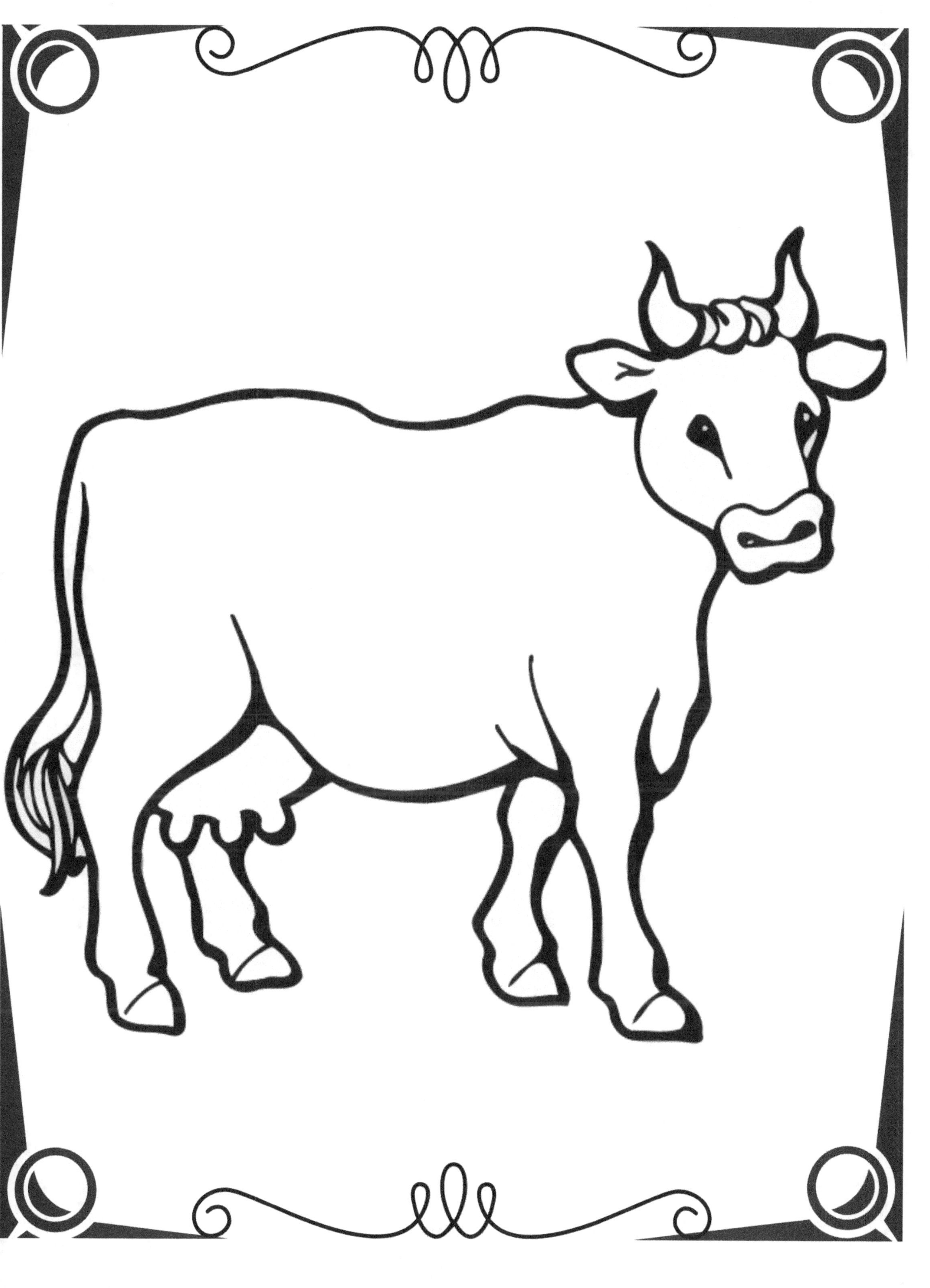

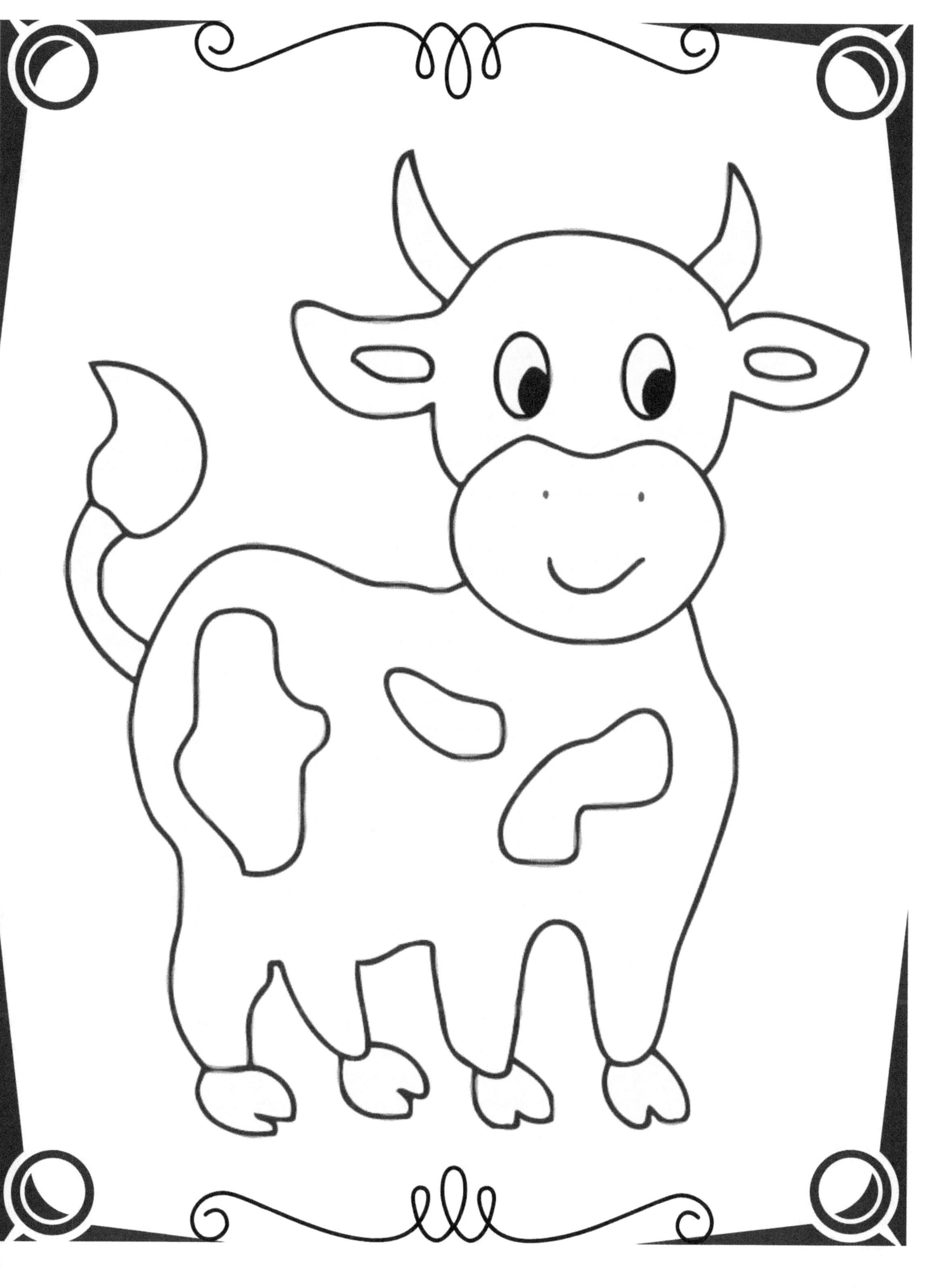

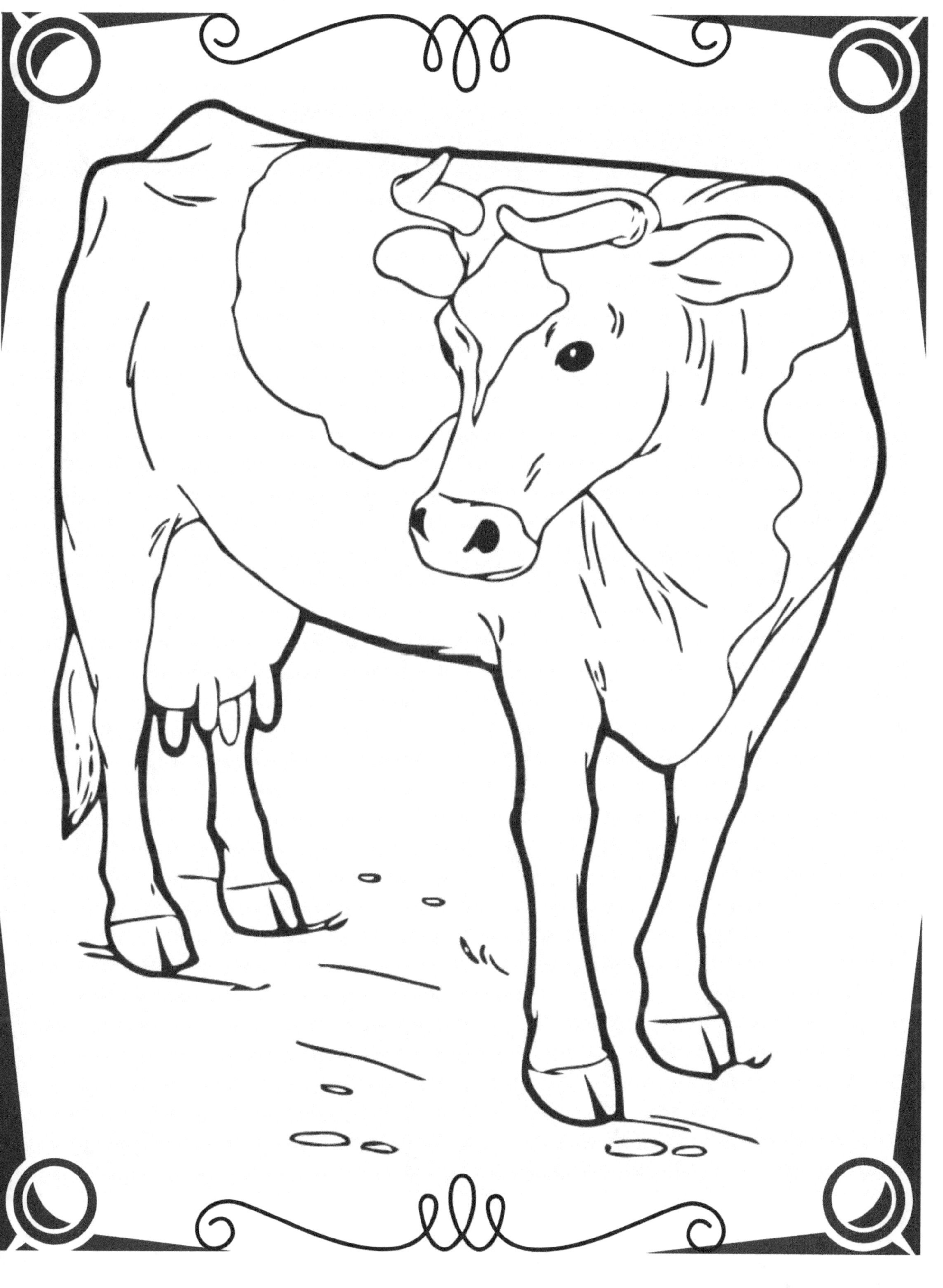

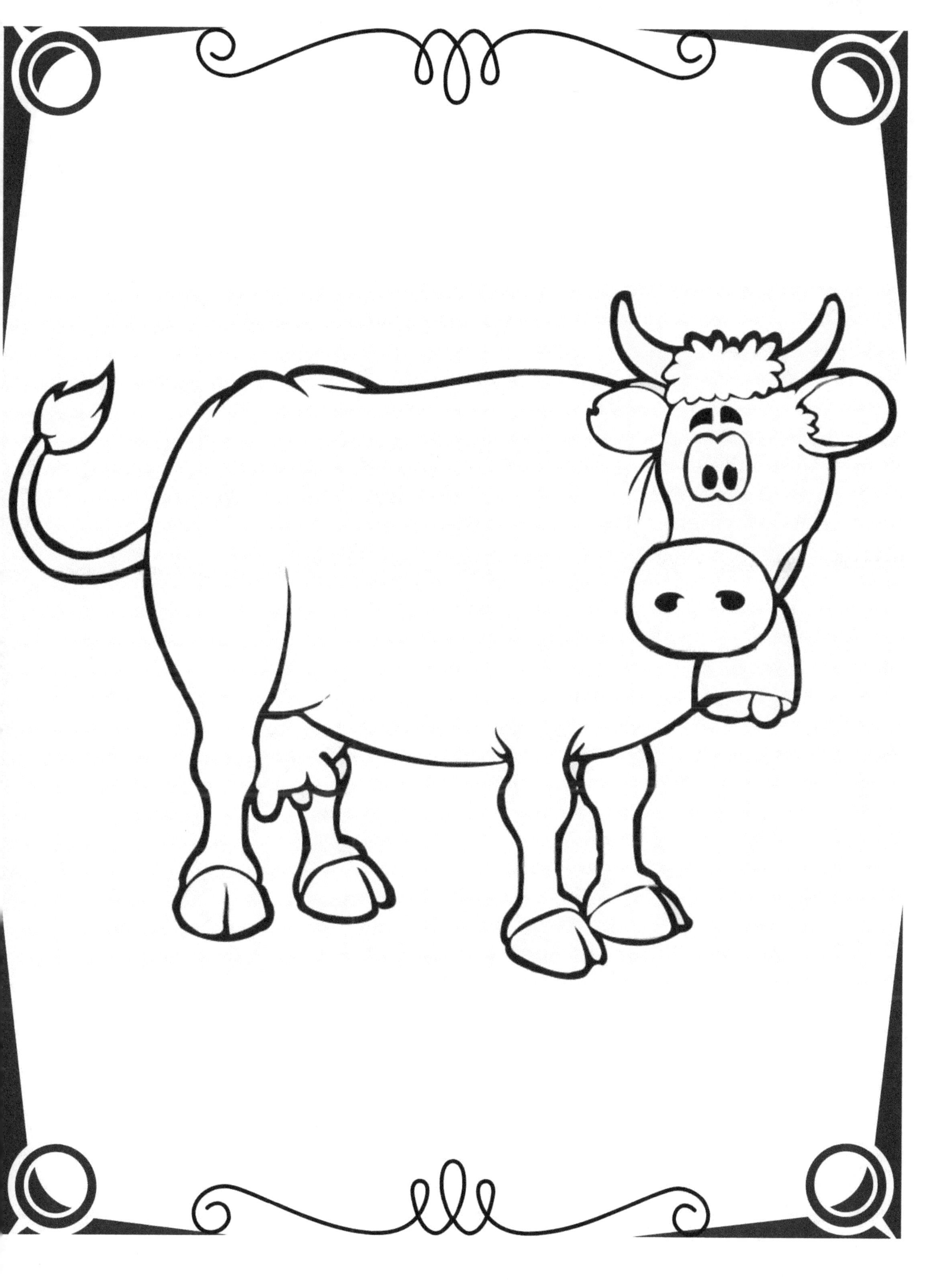

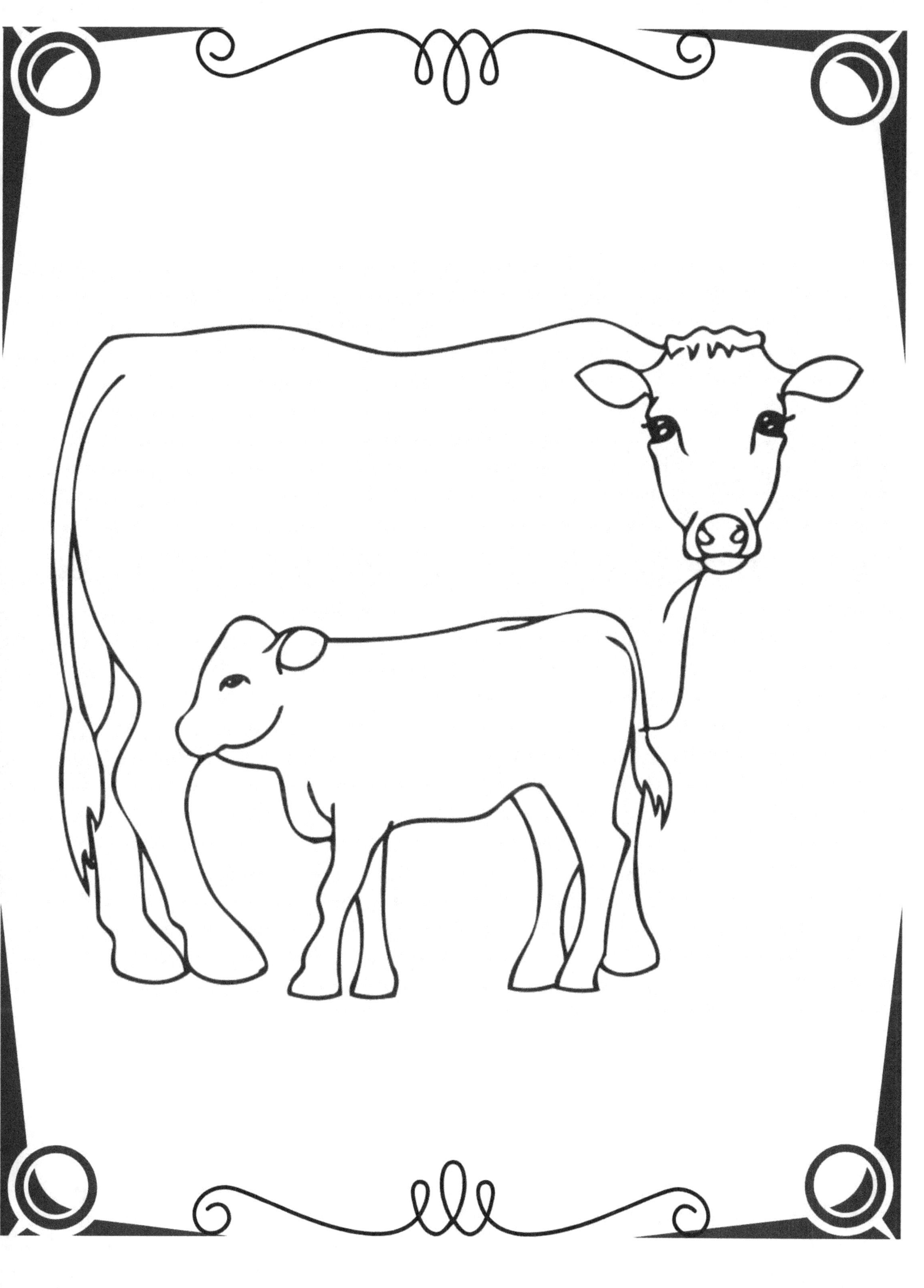

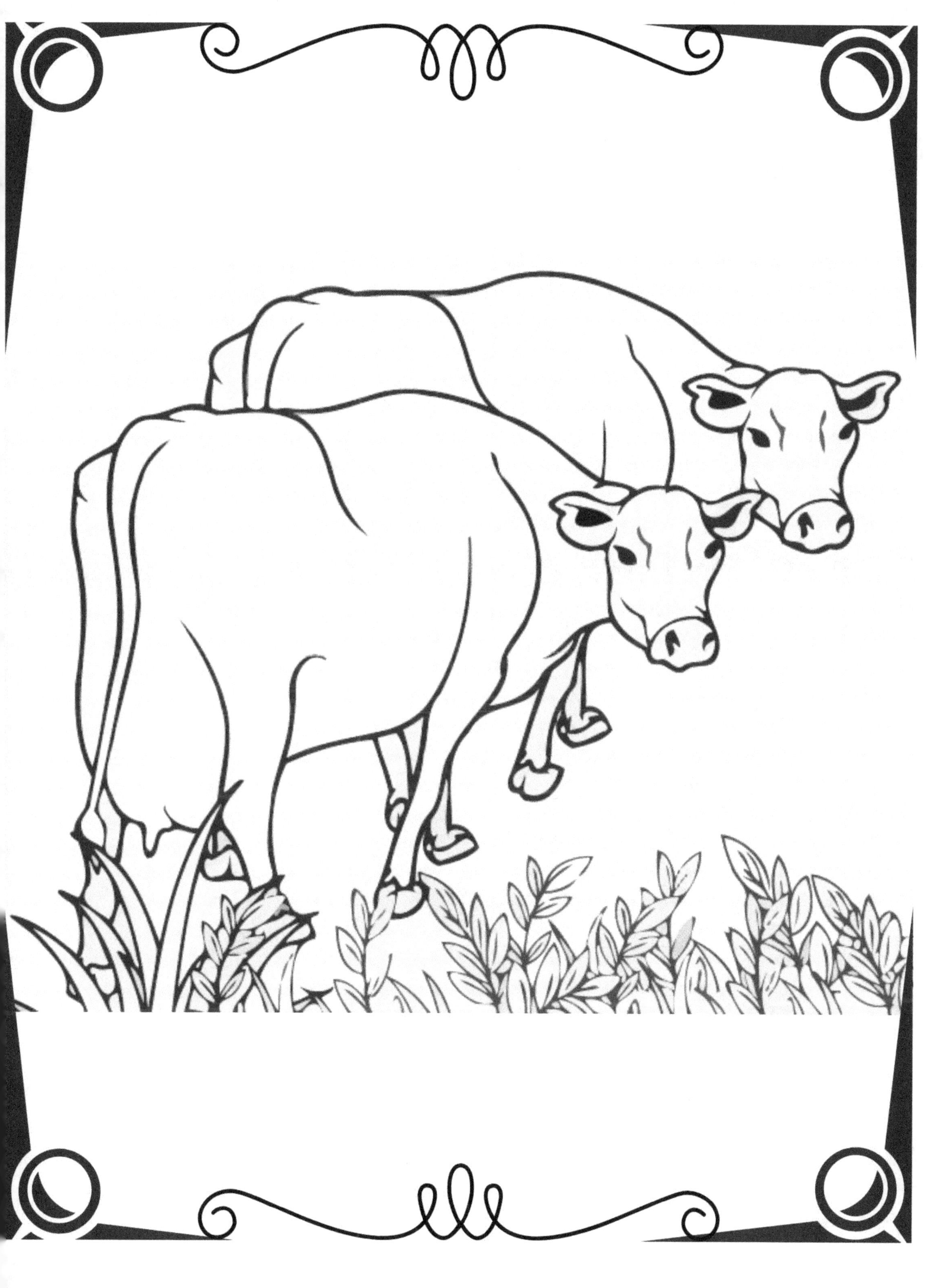

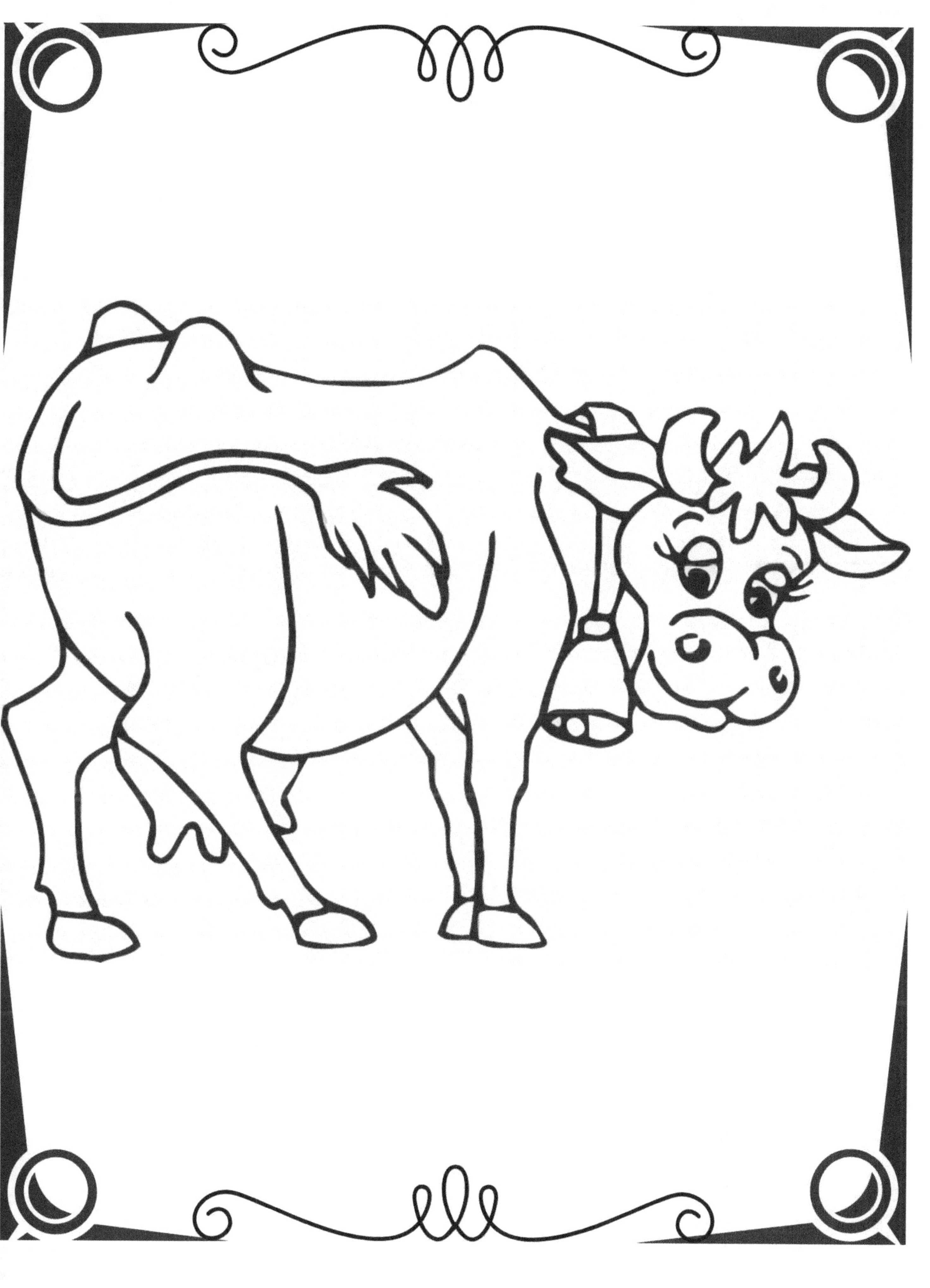

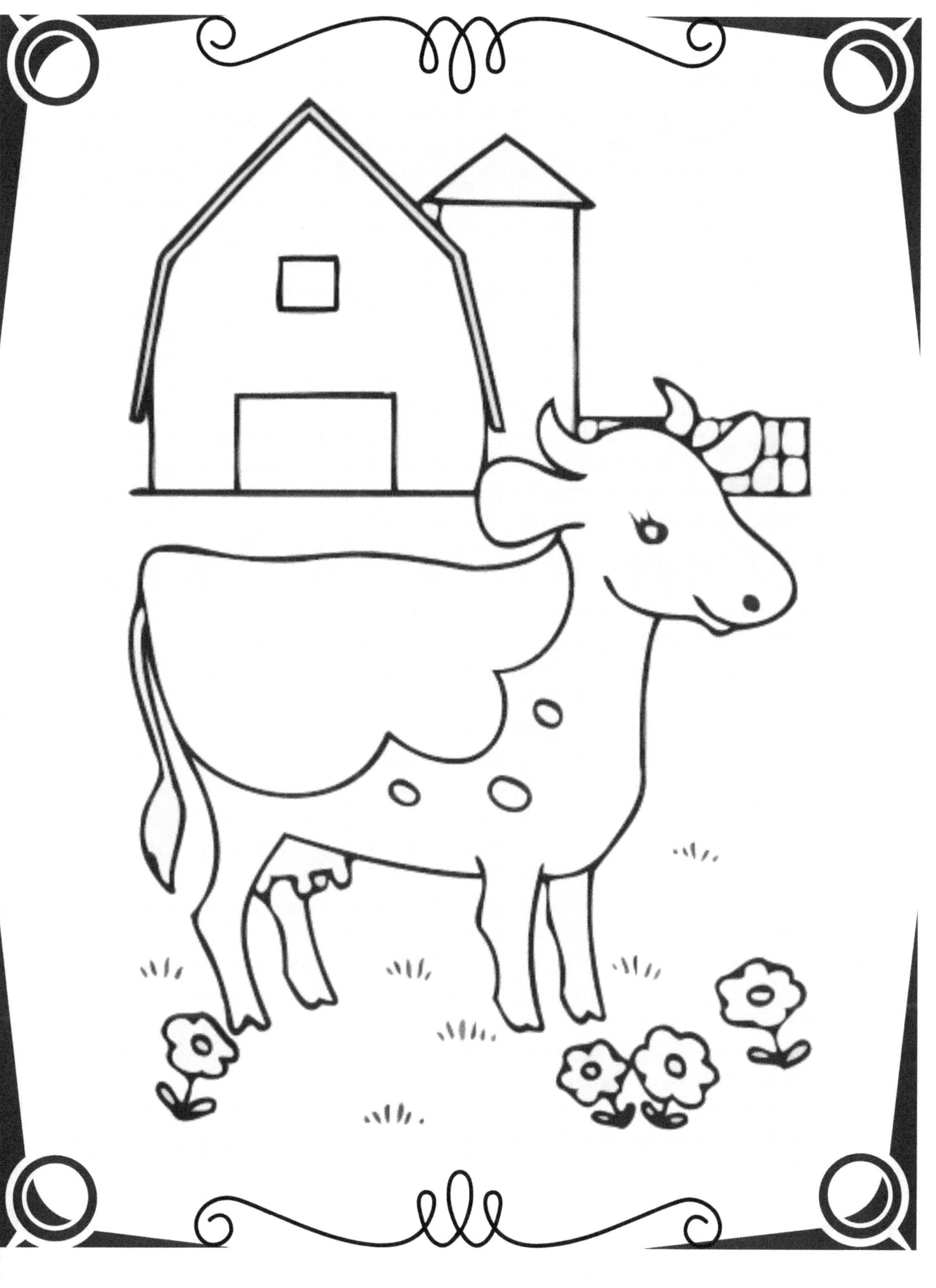

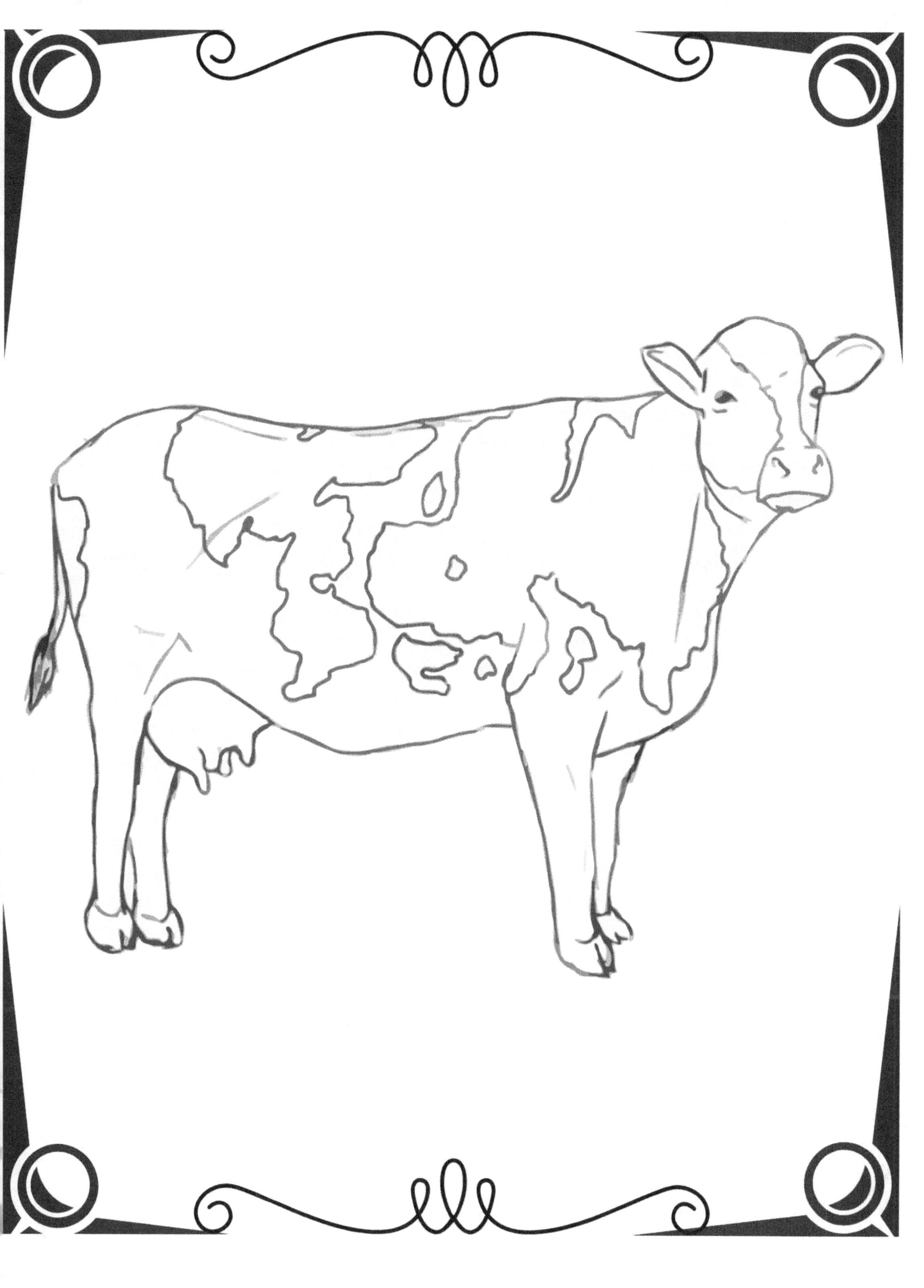

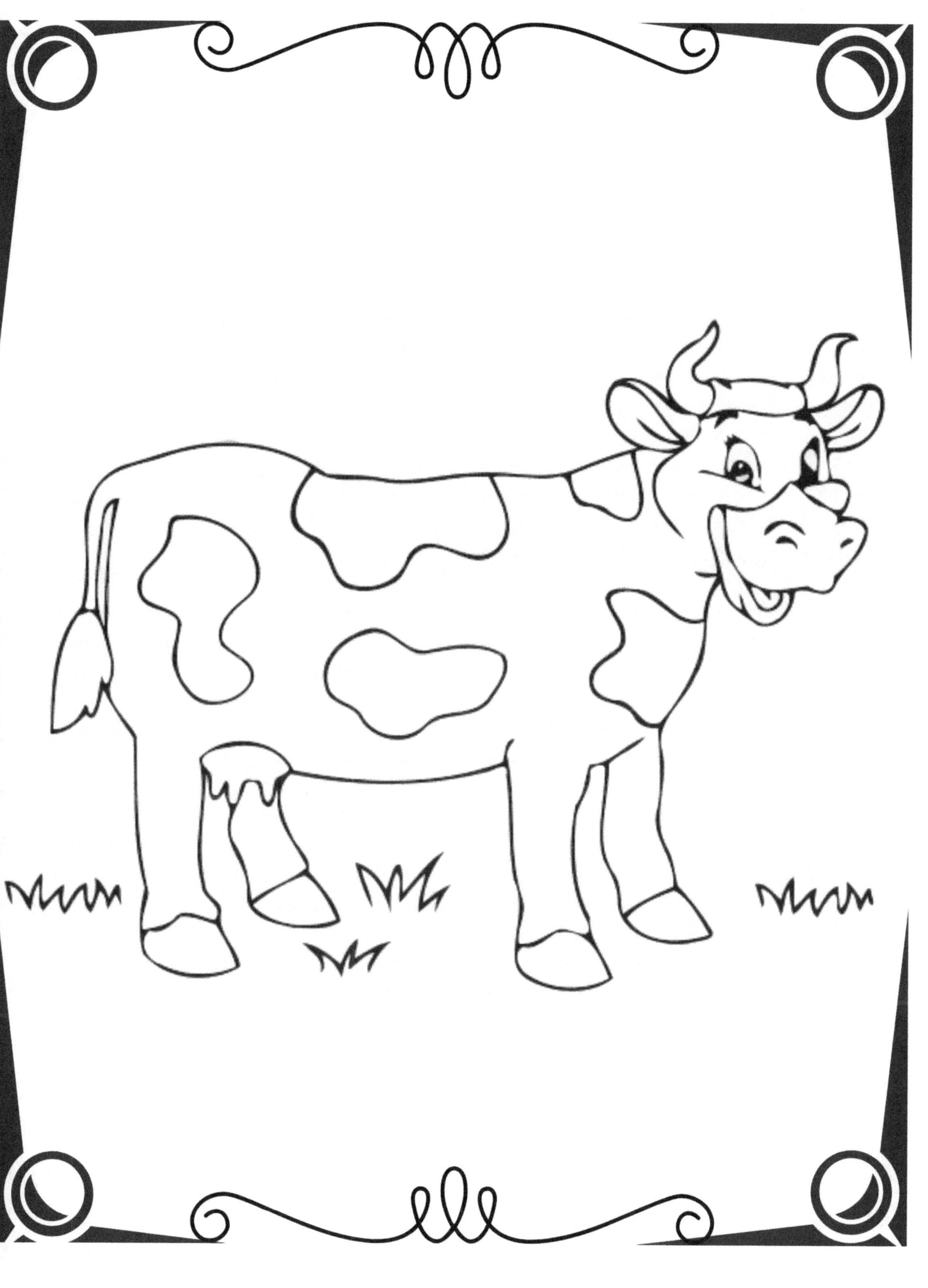

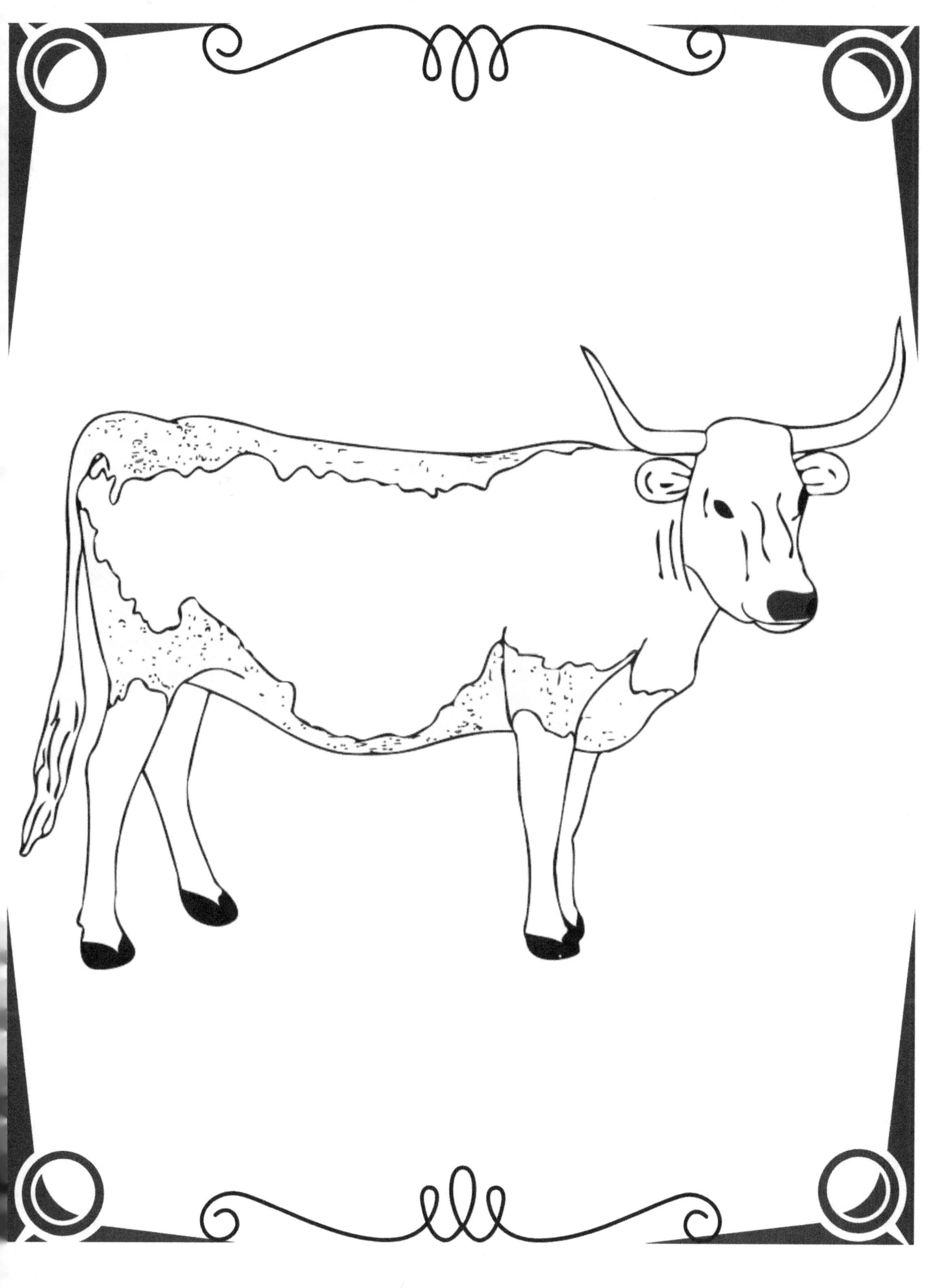

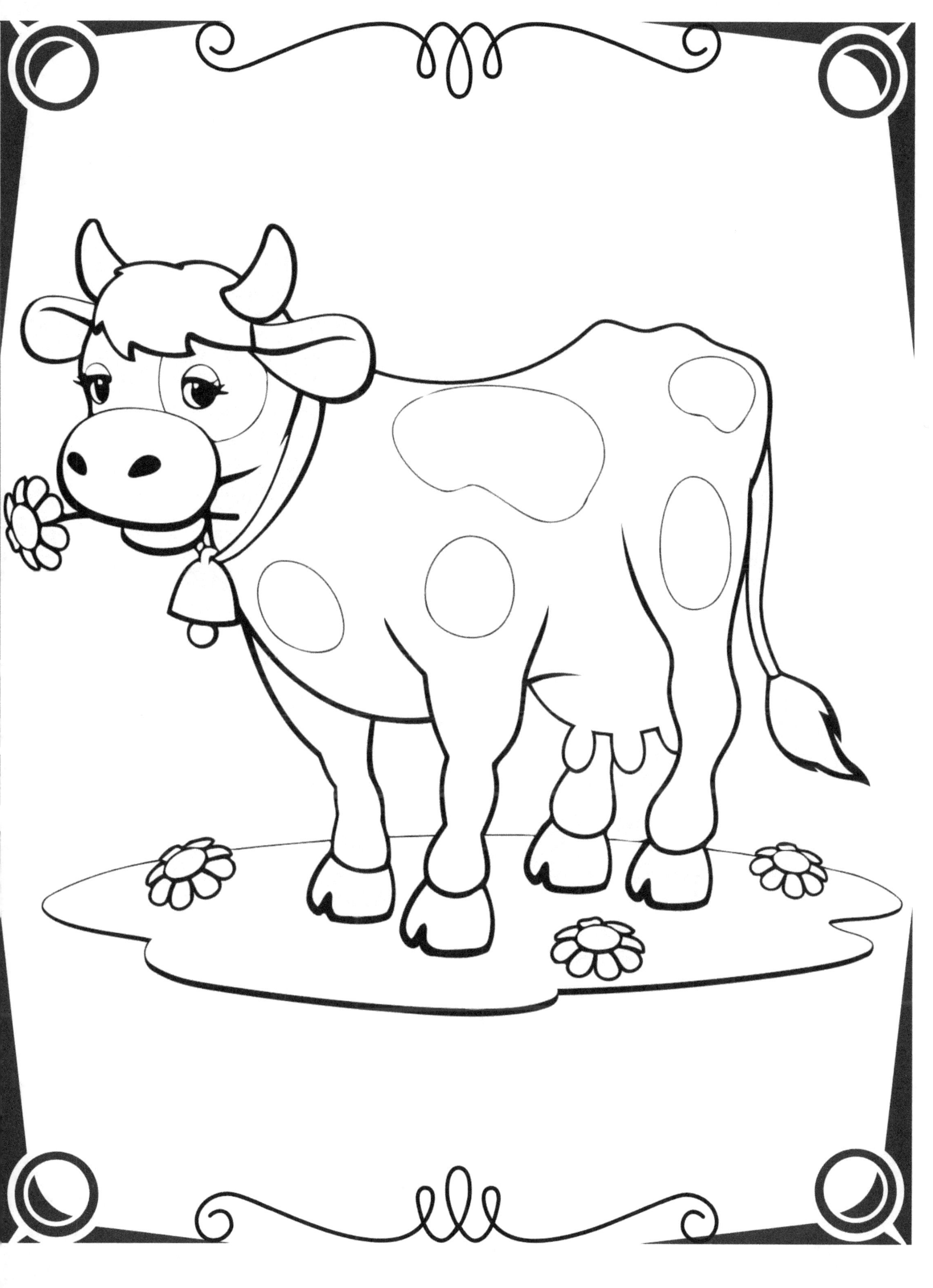

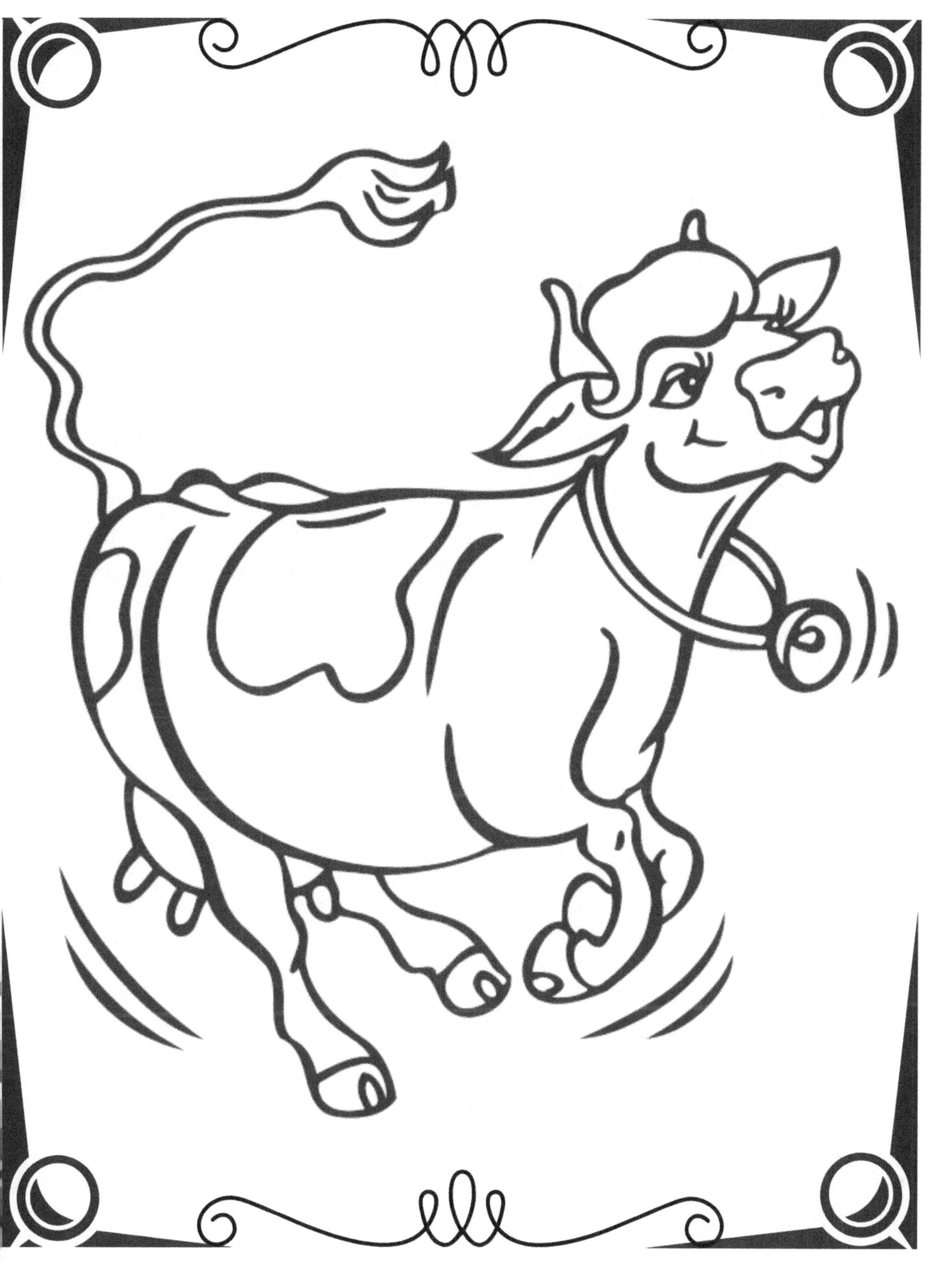

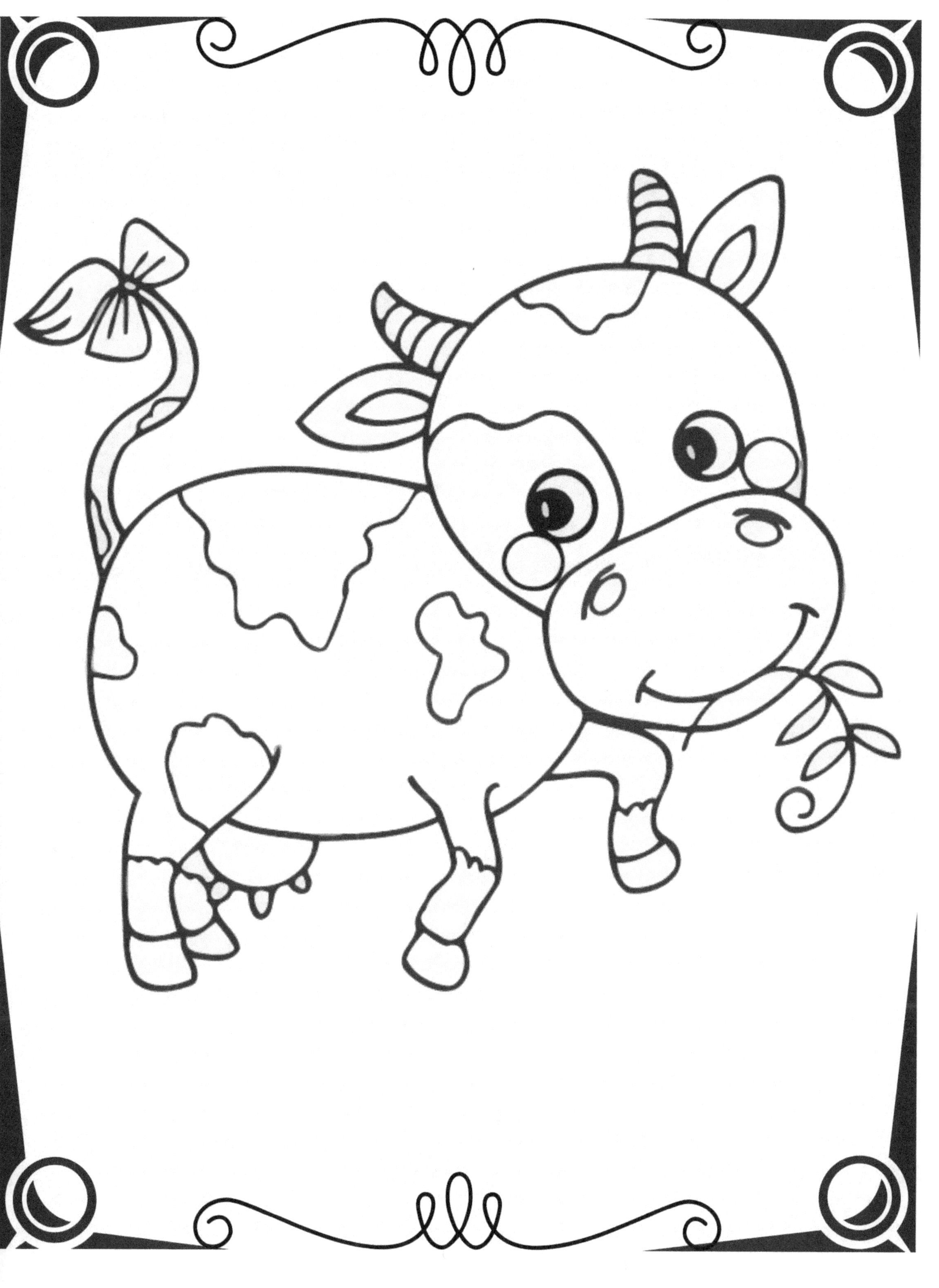

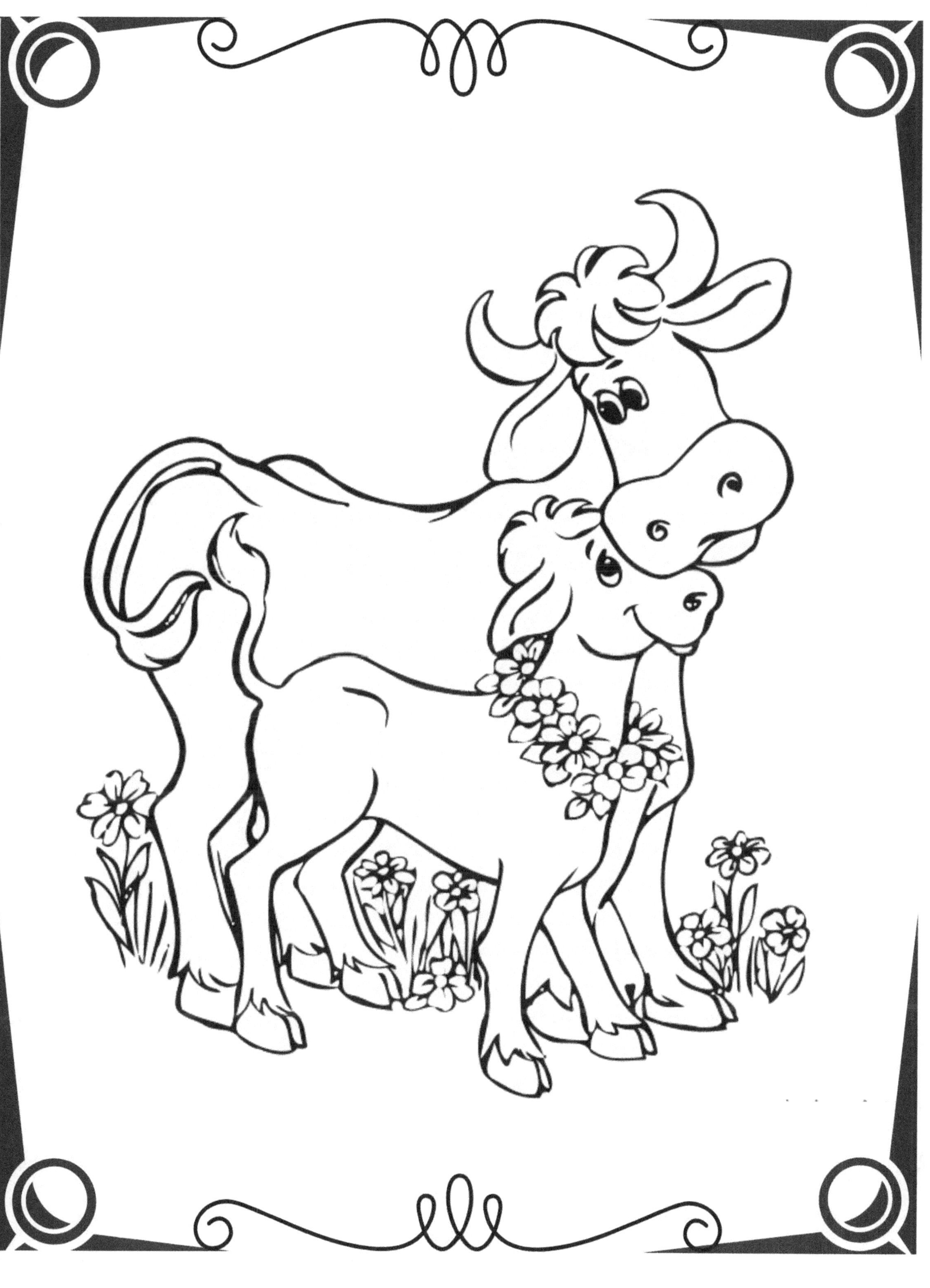

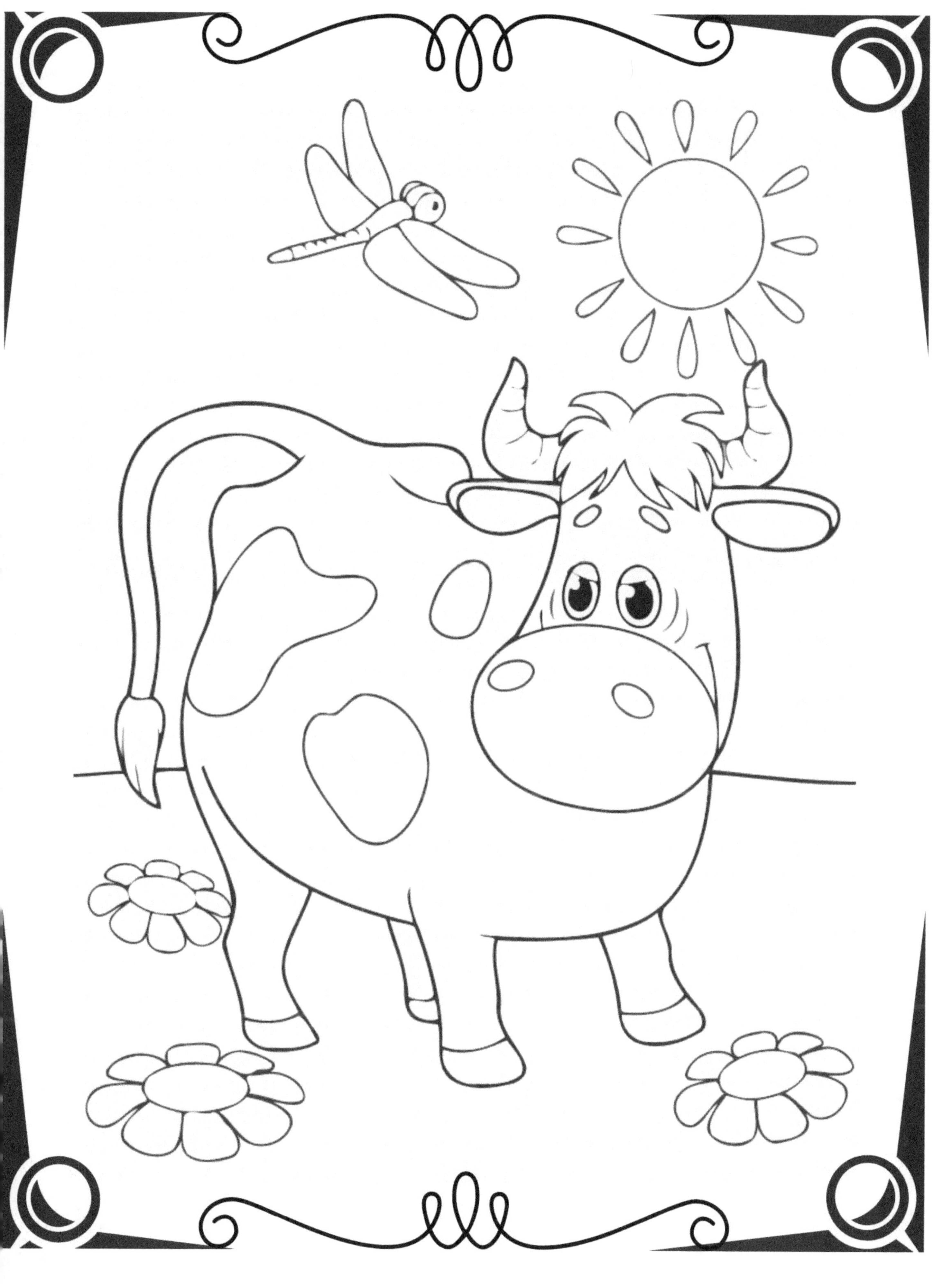

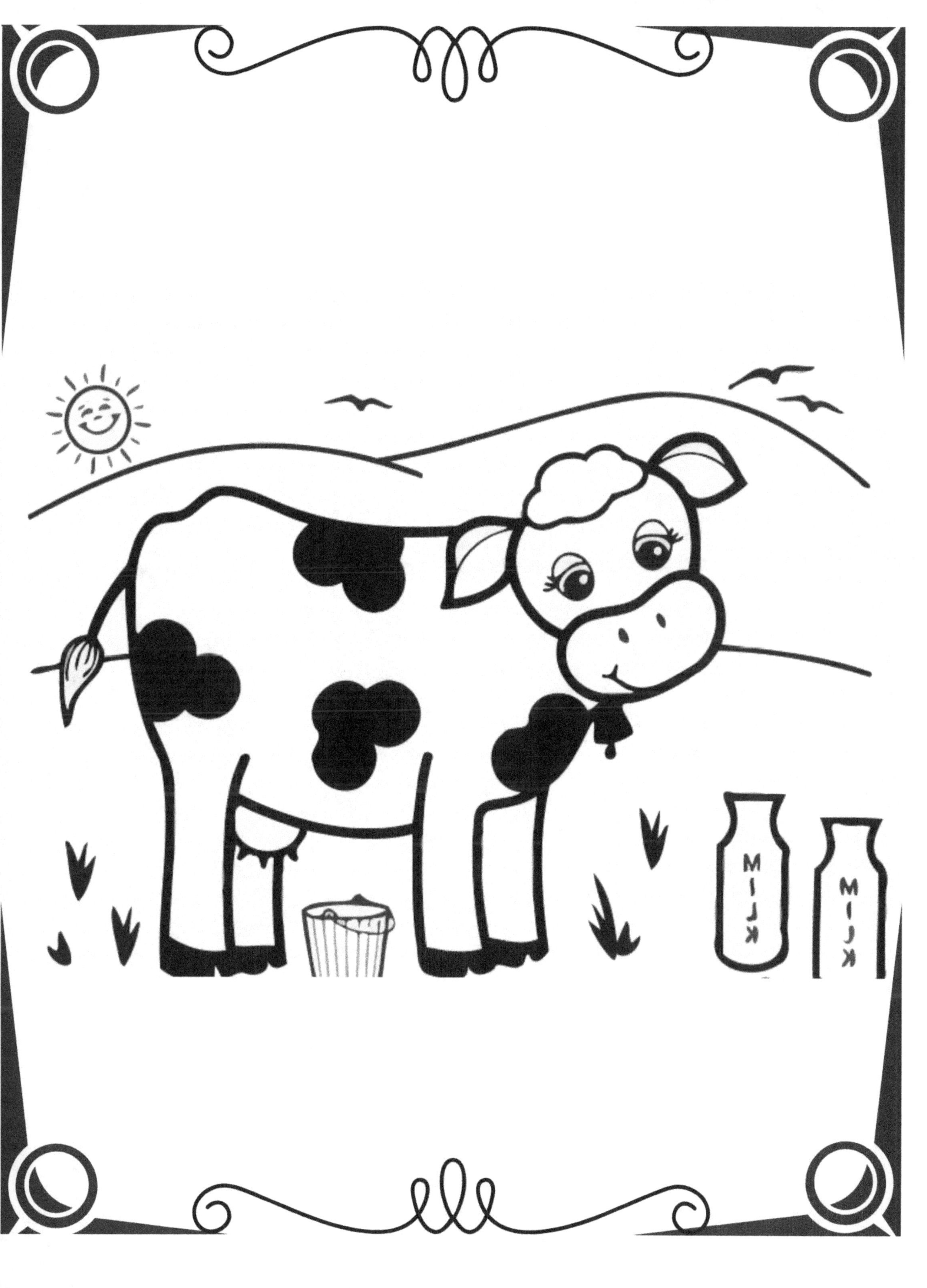
MILK
MILK

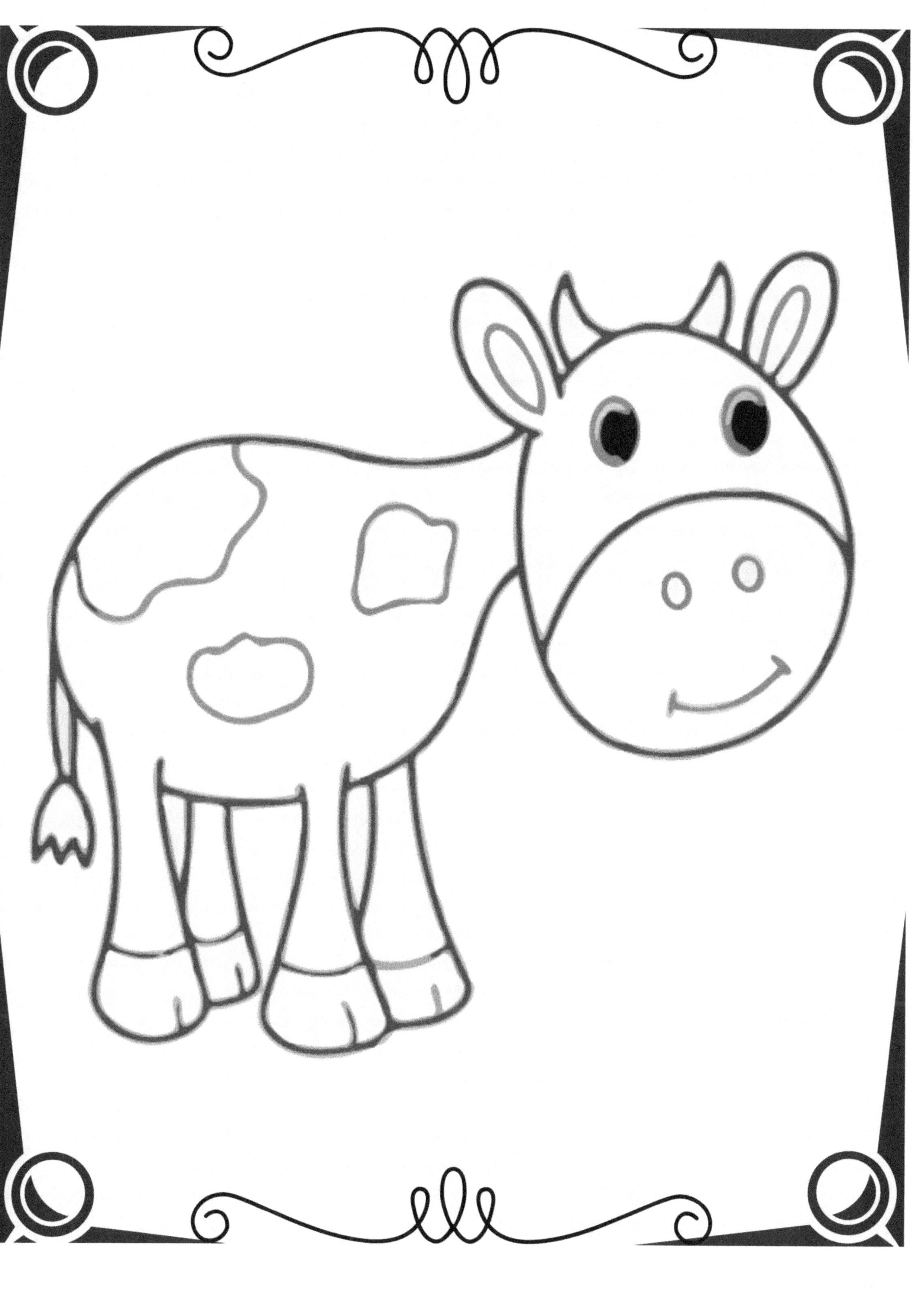

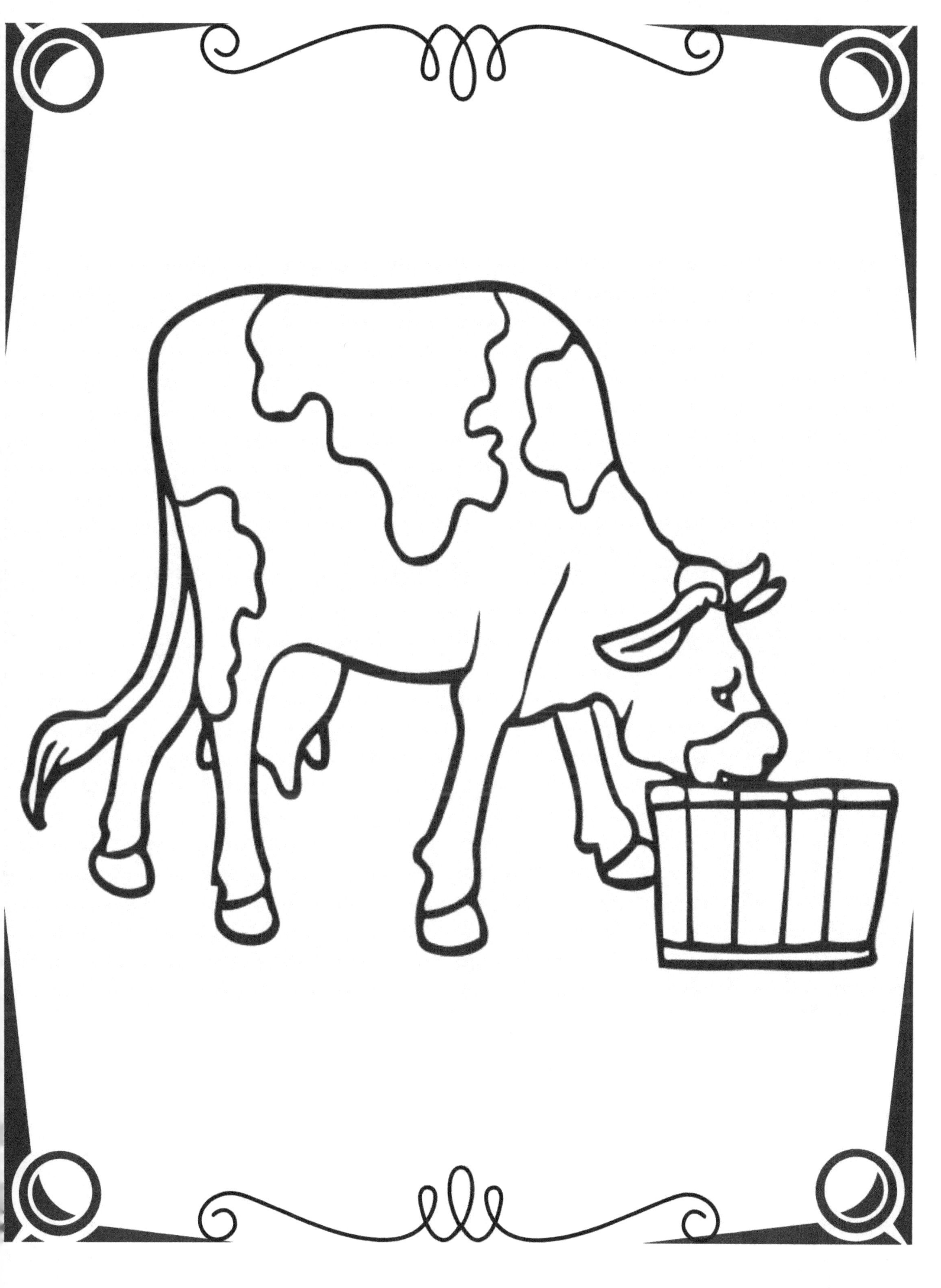

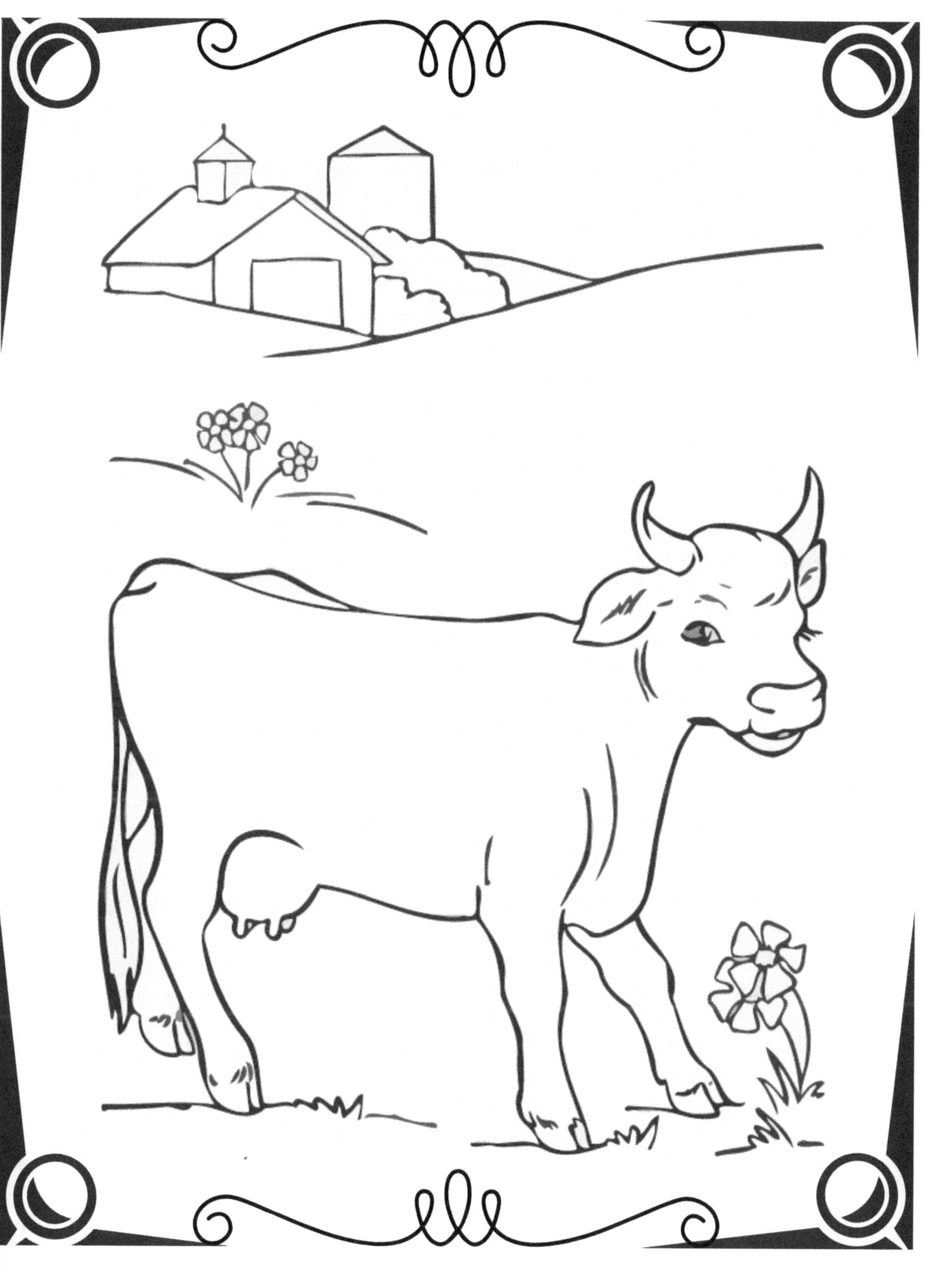

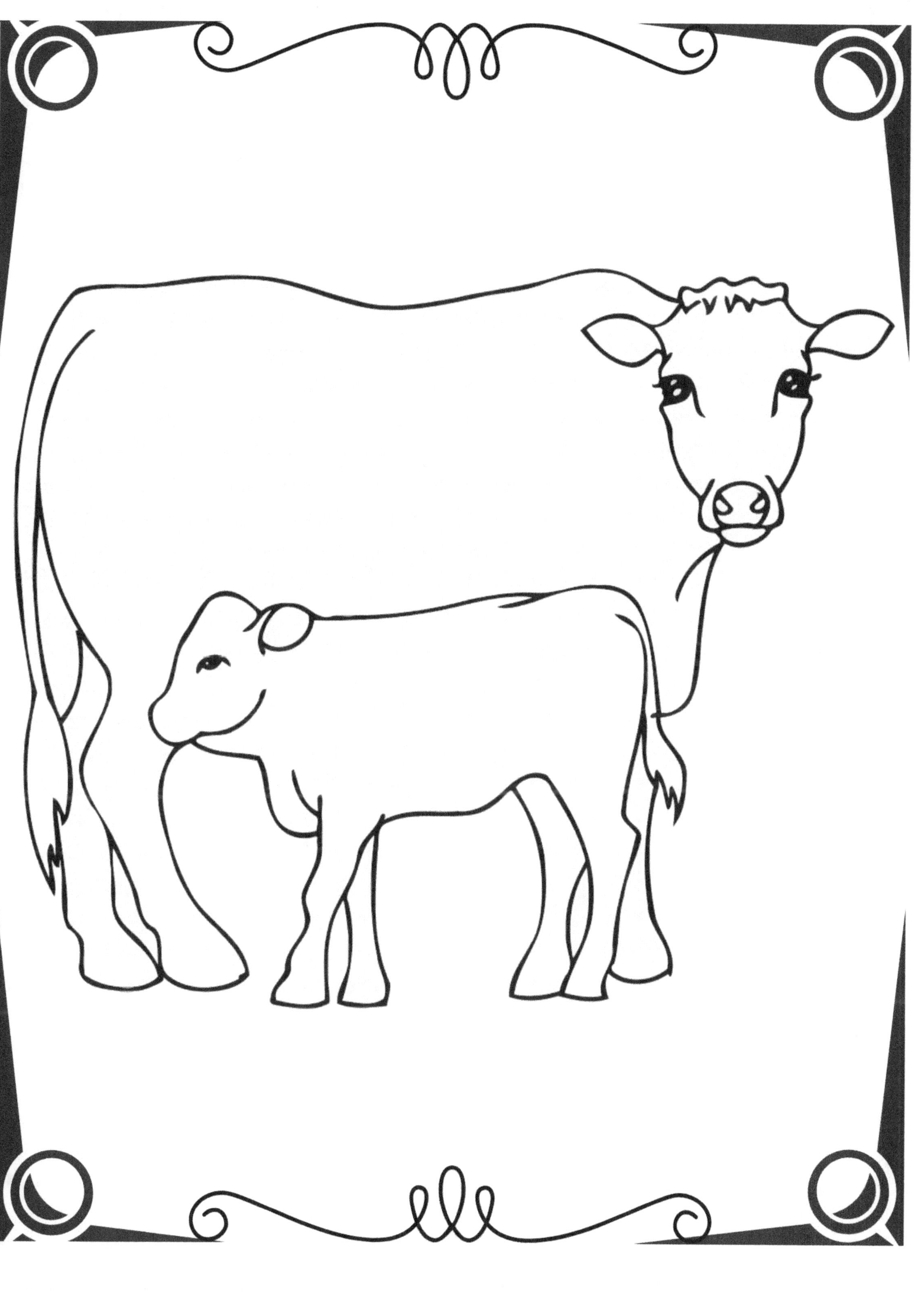

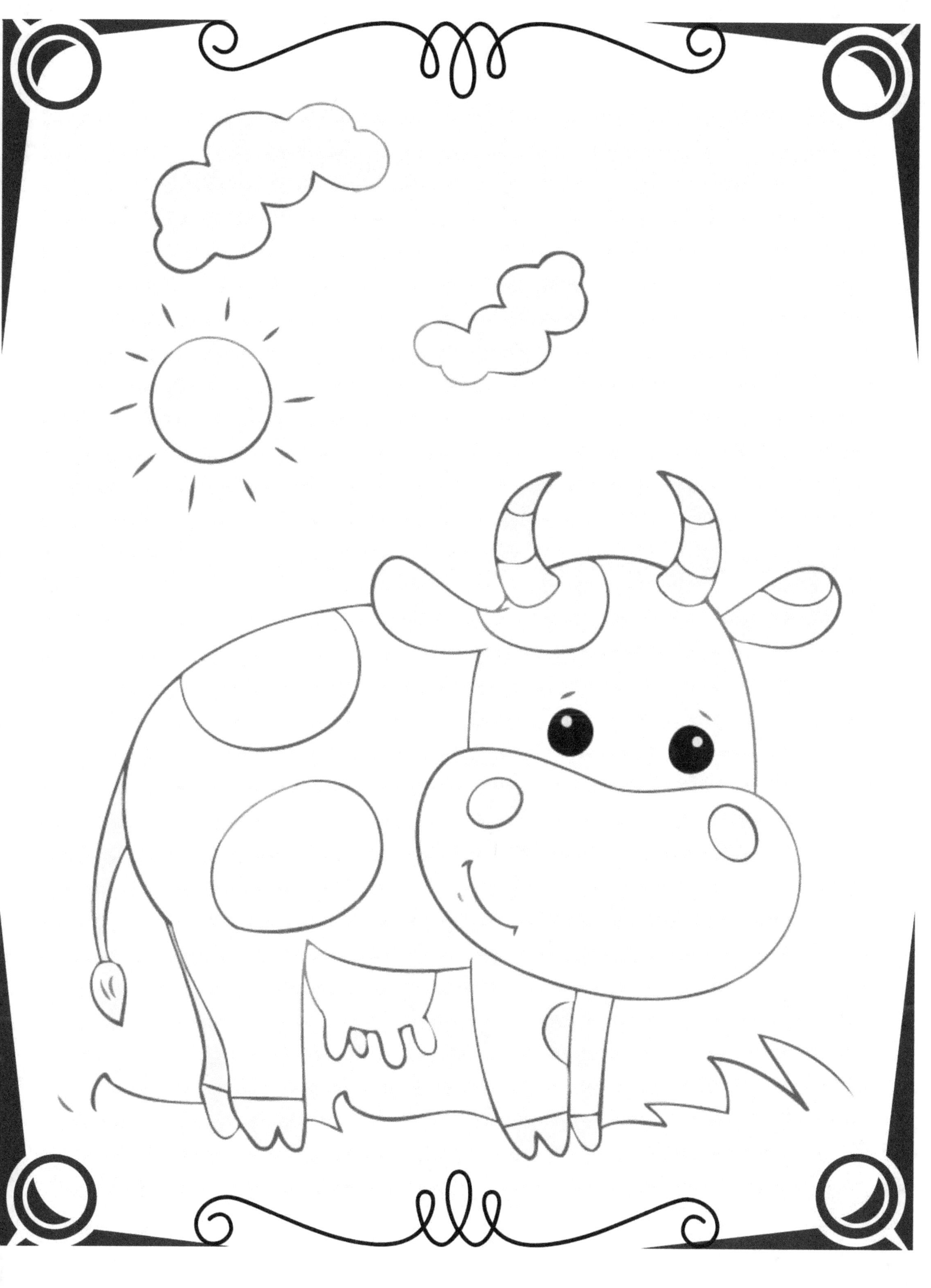

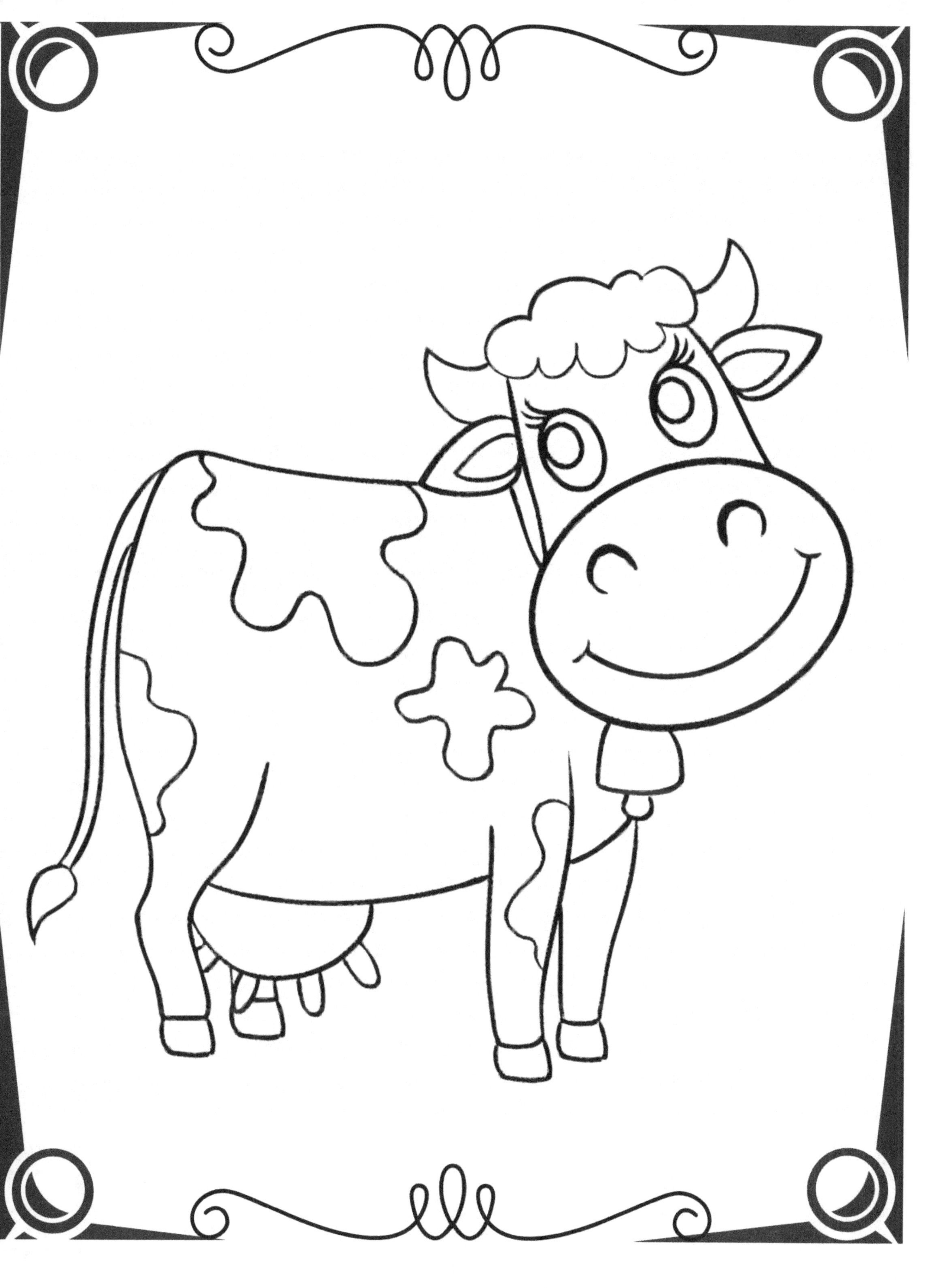

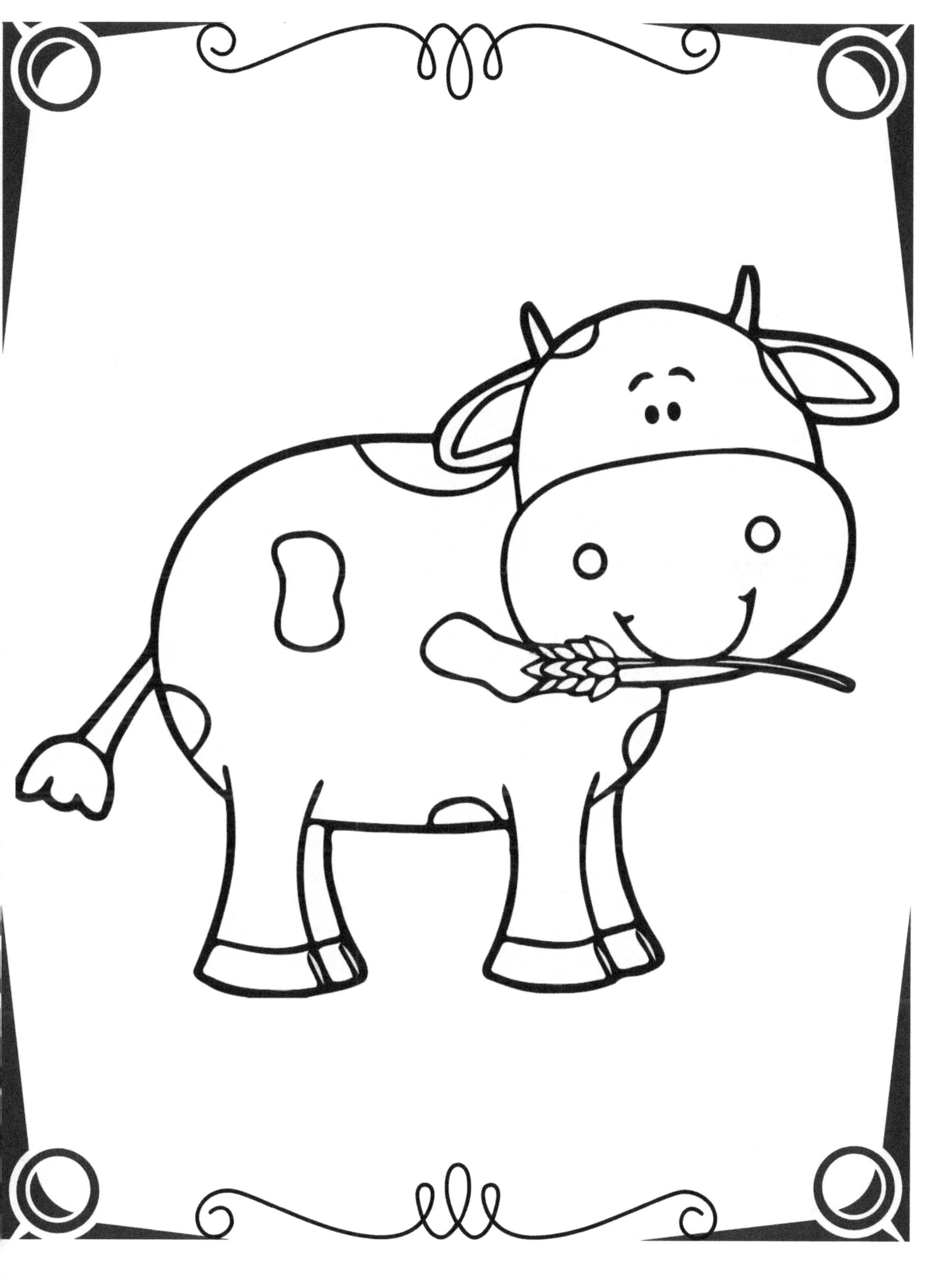

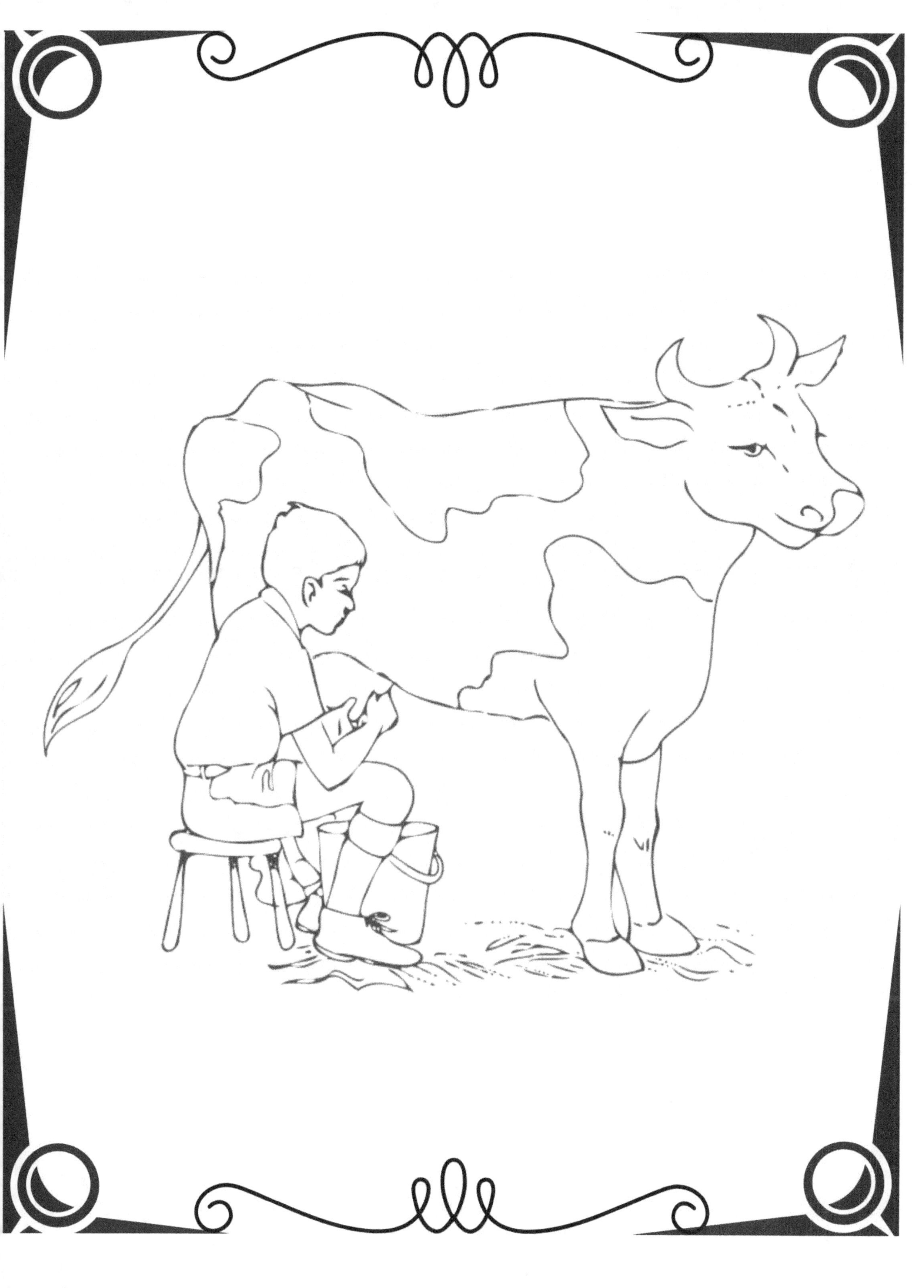

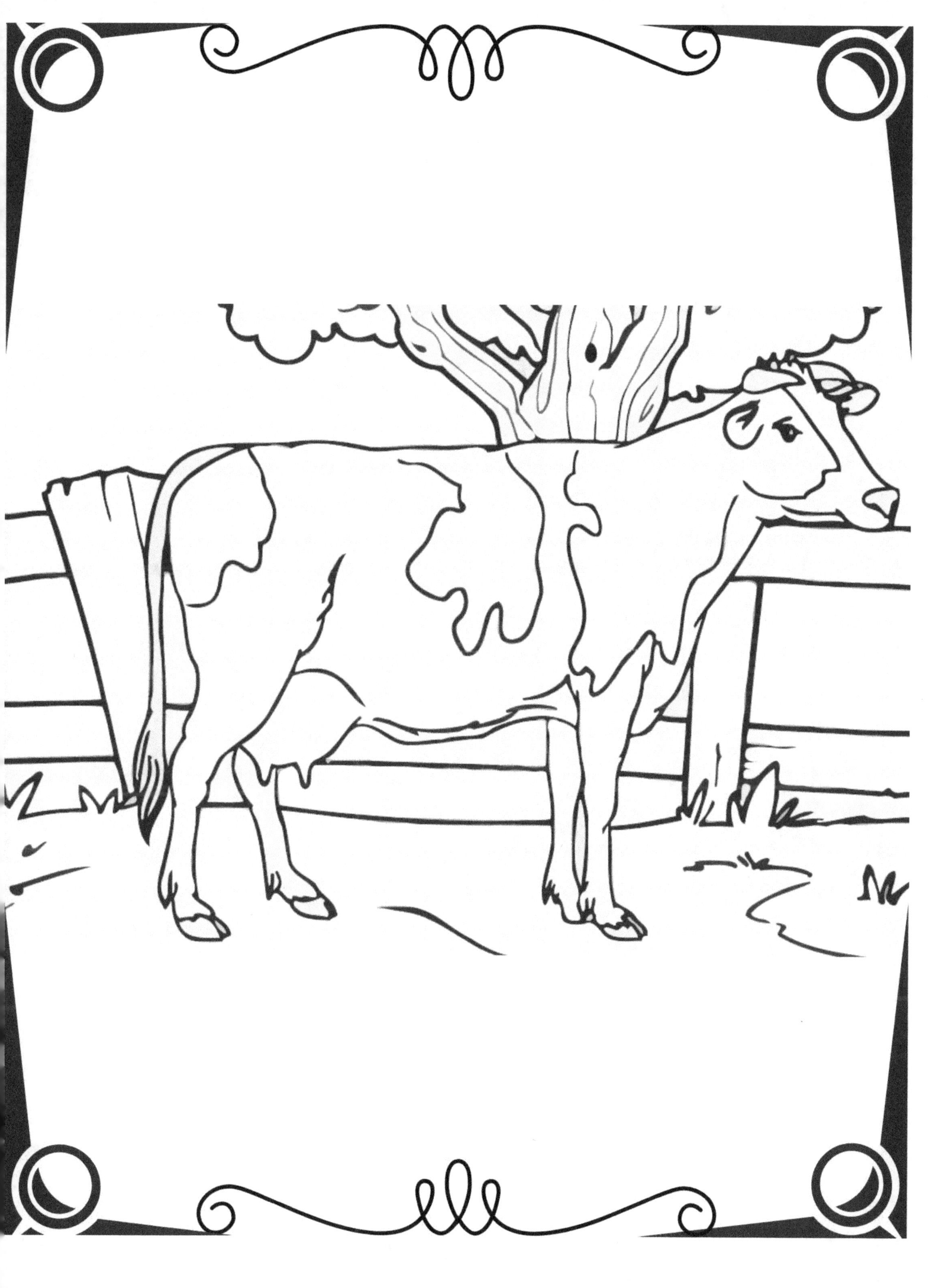

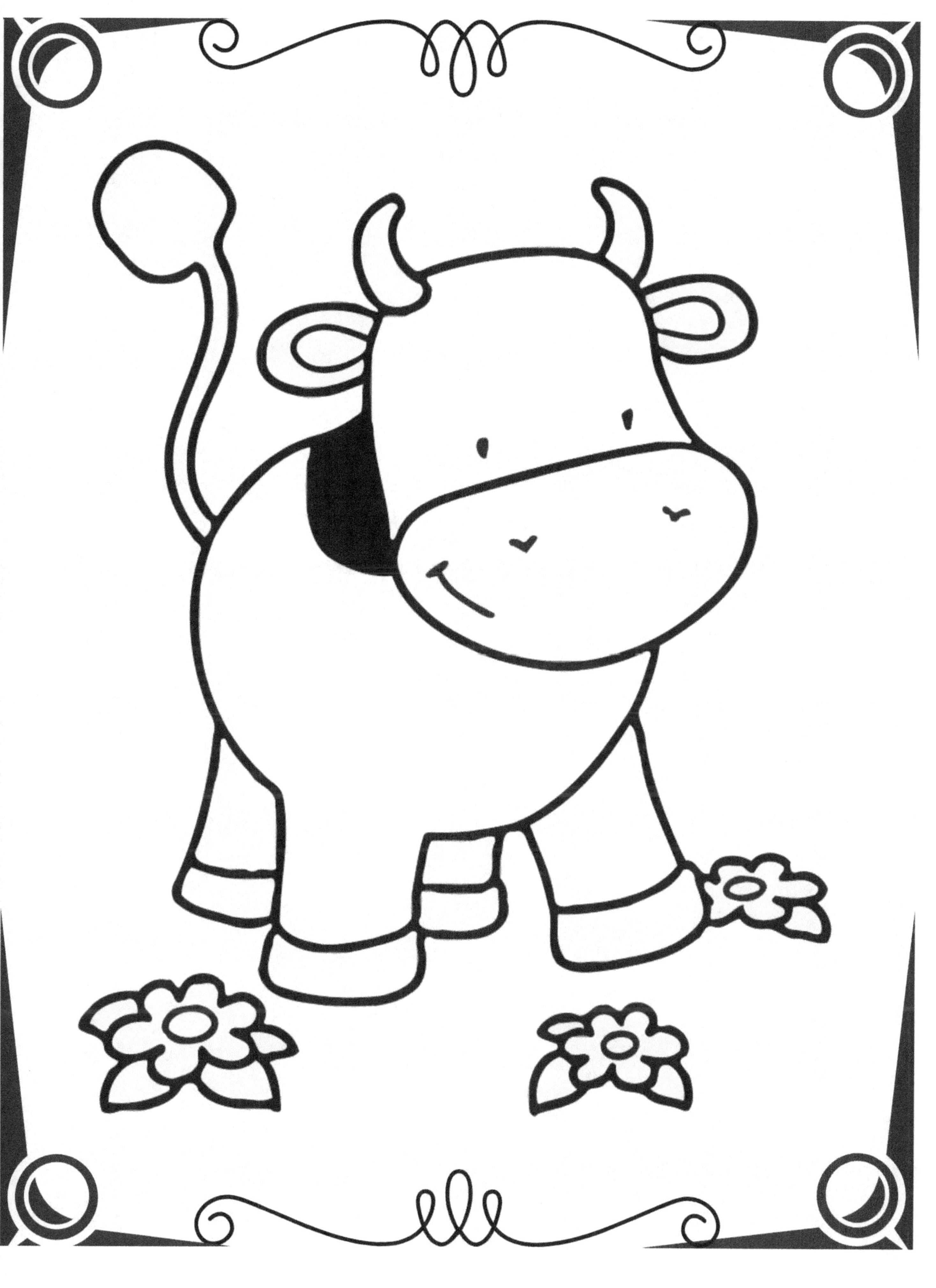

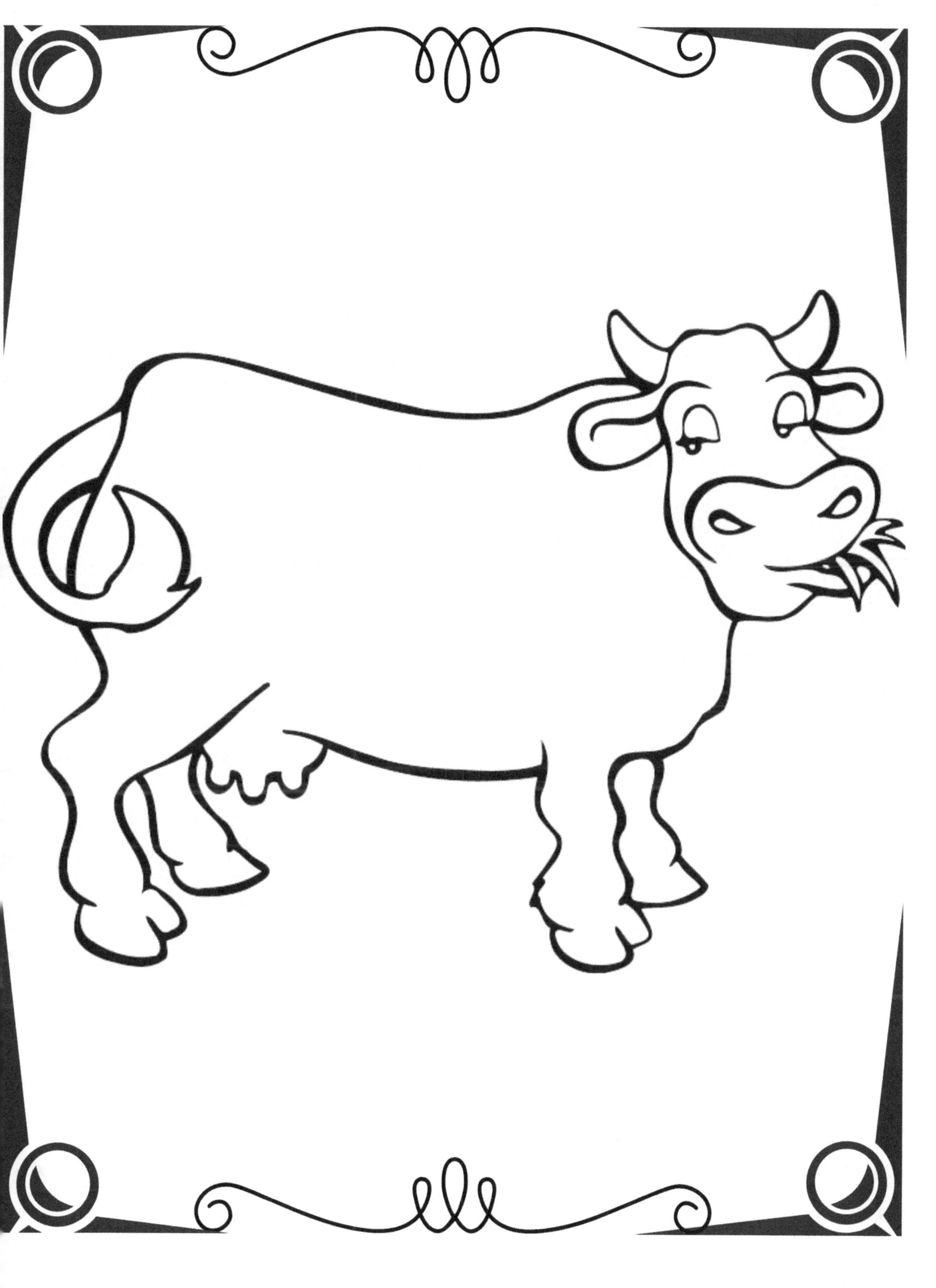

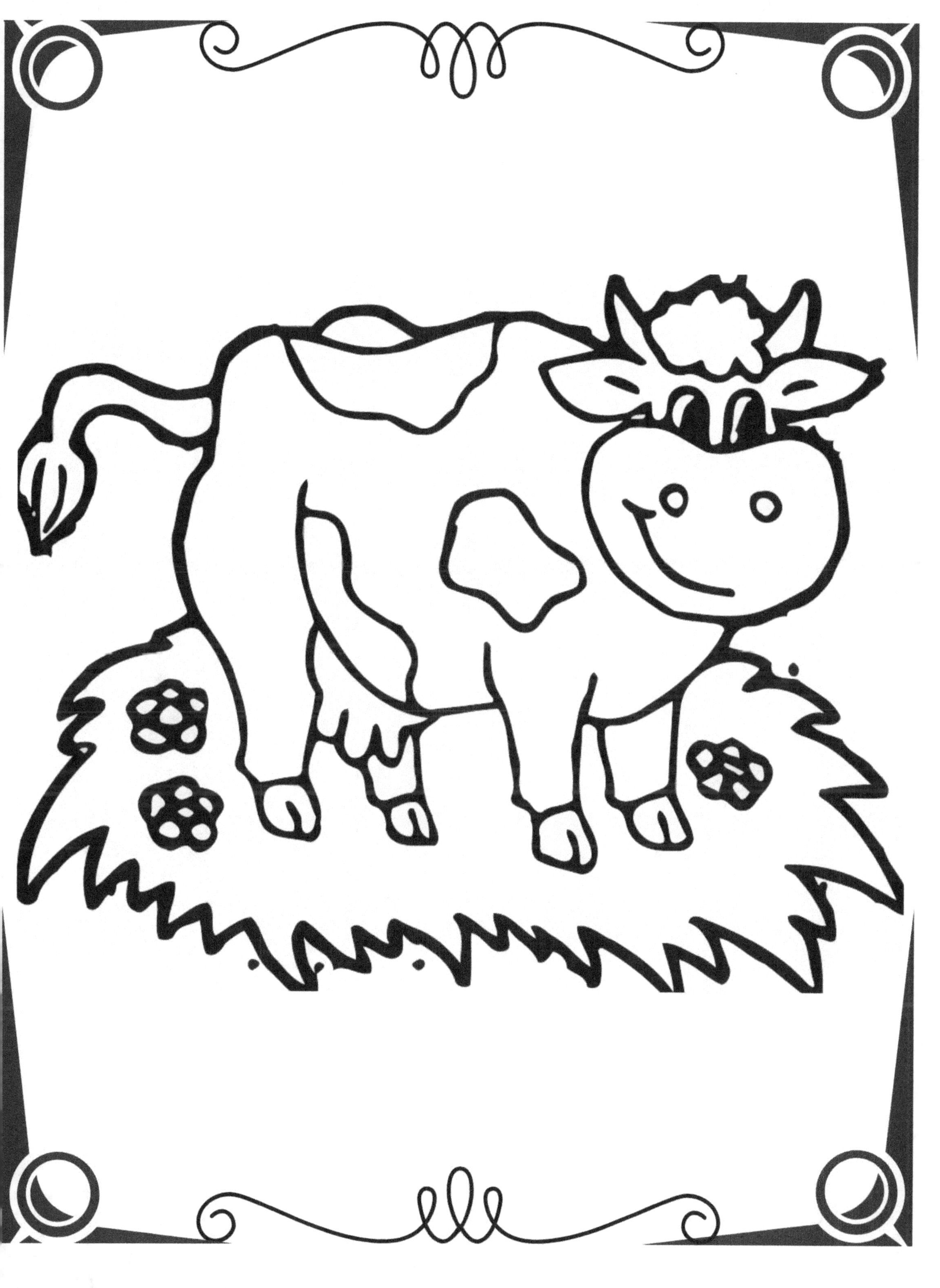

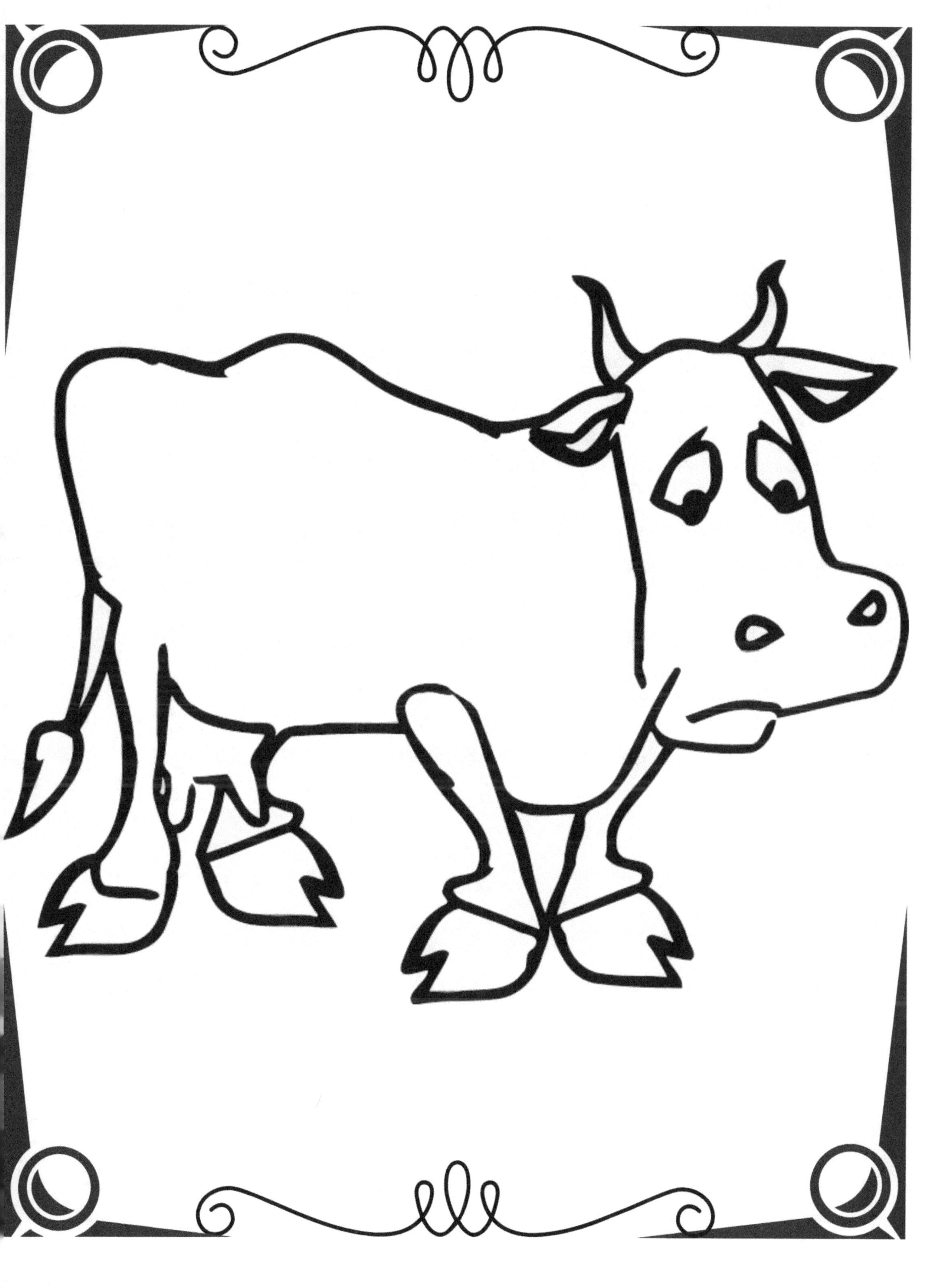

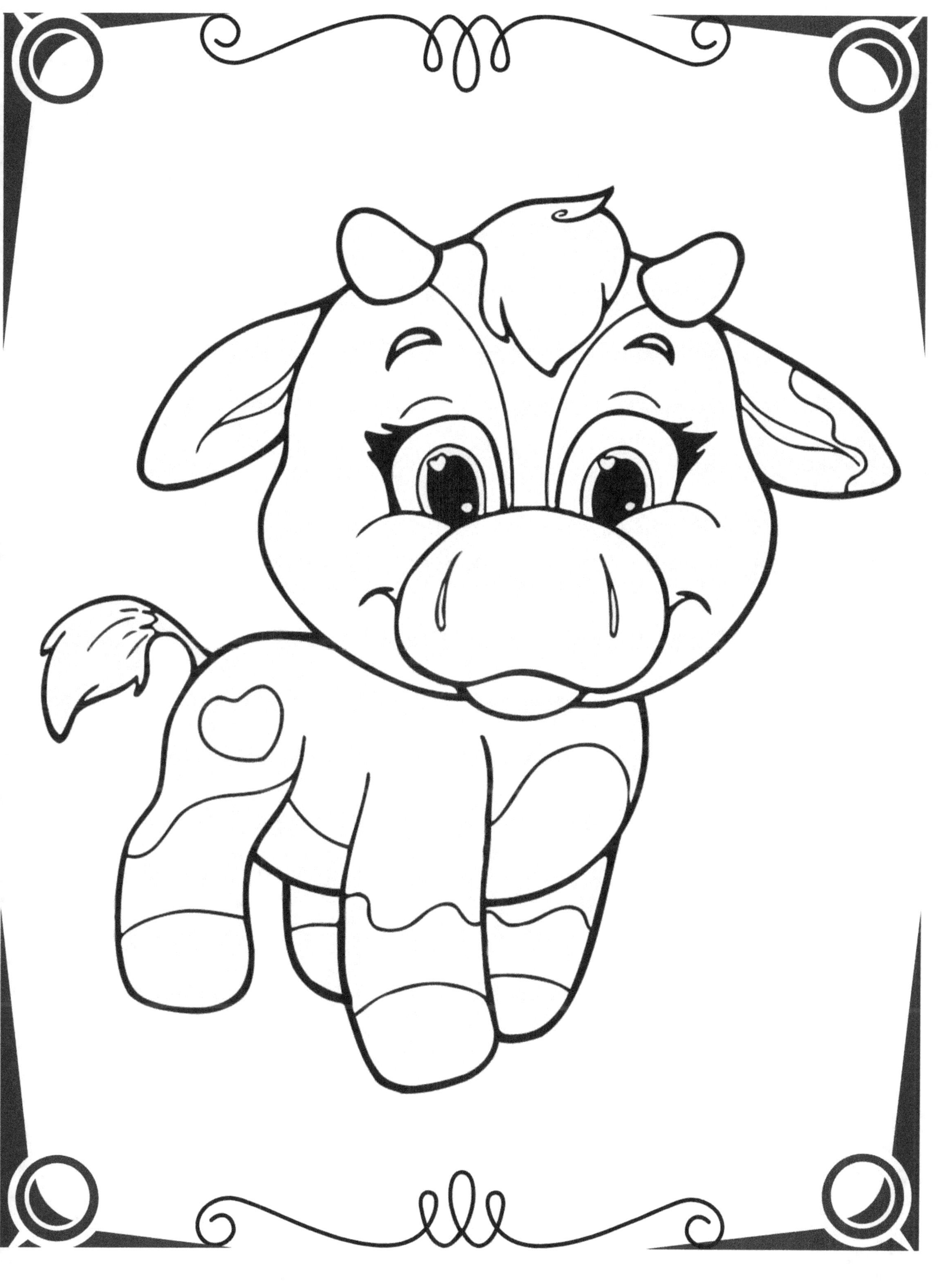

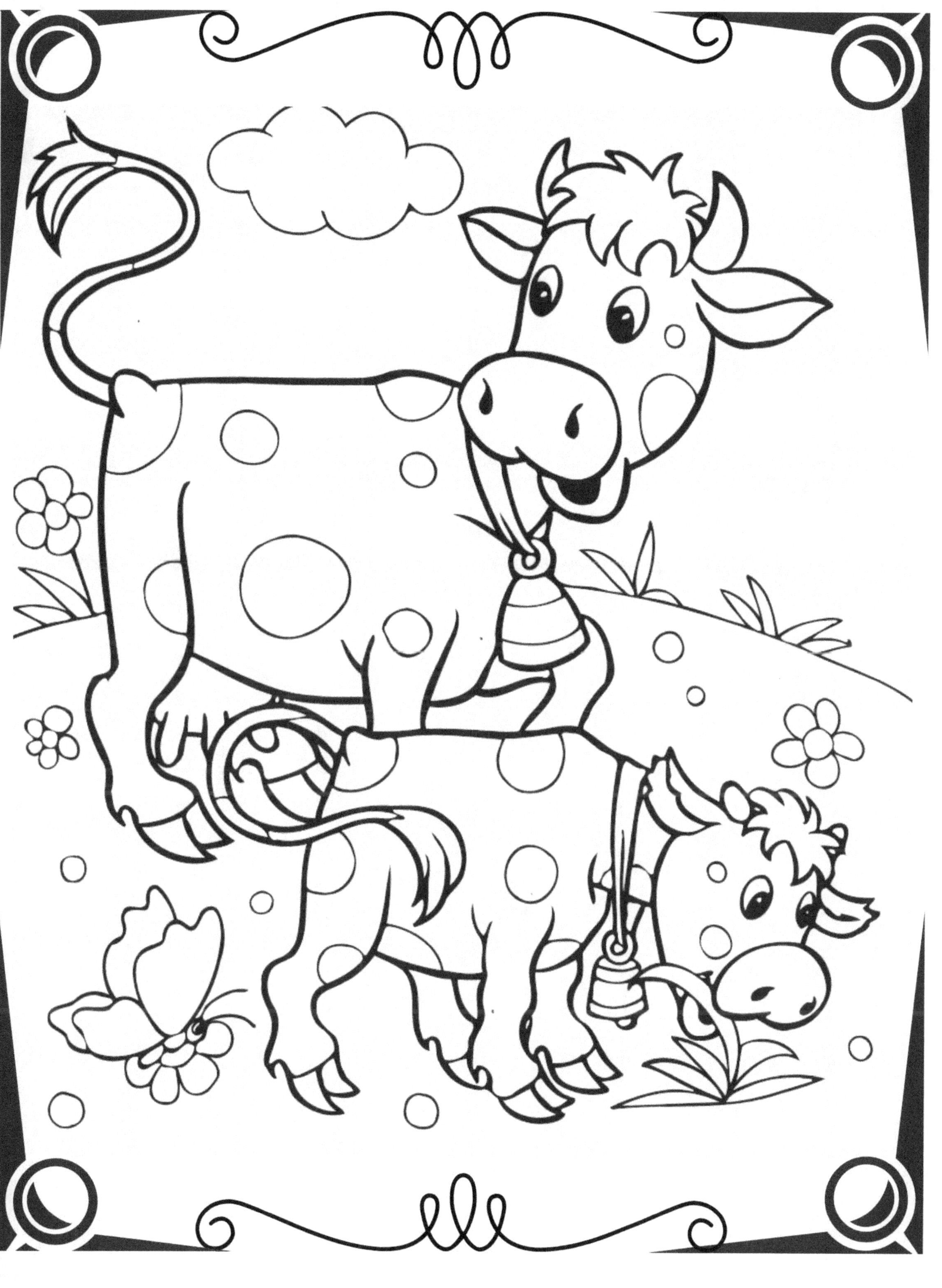

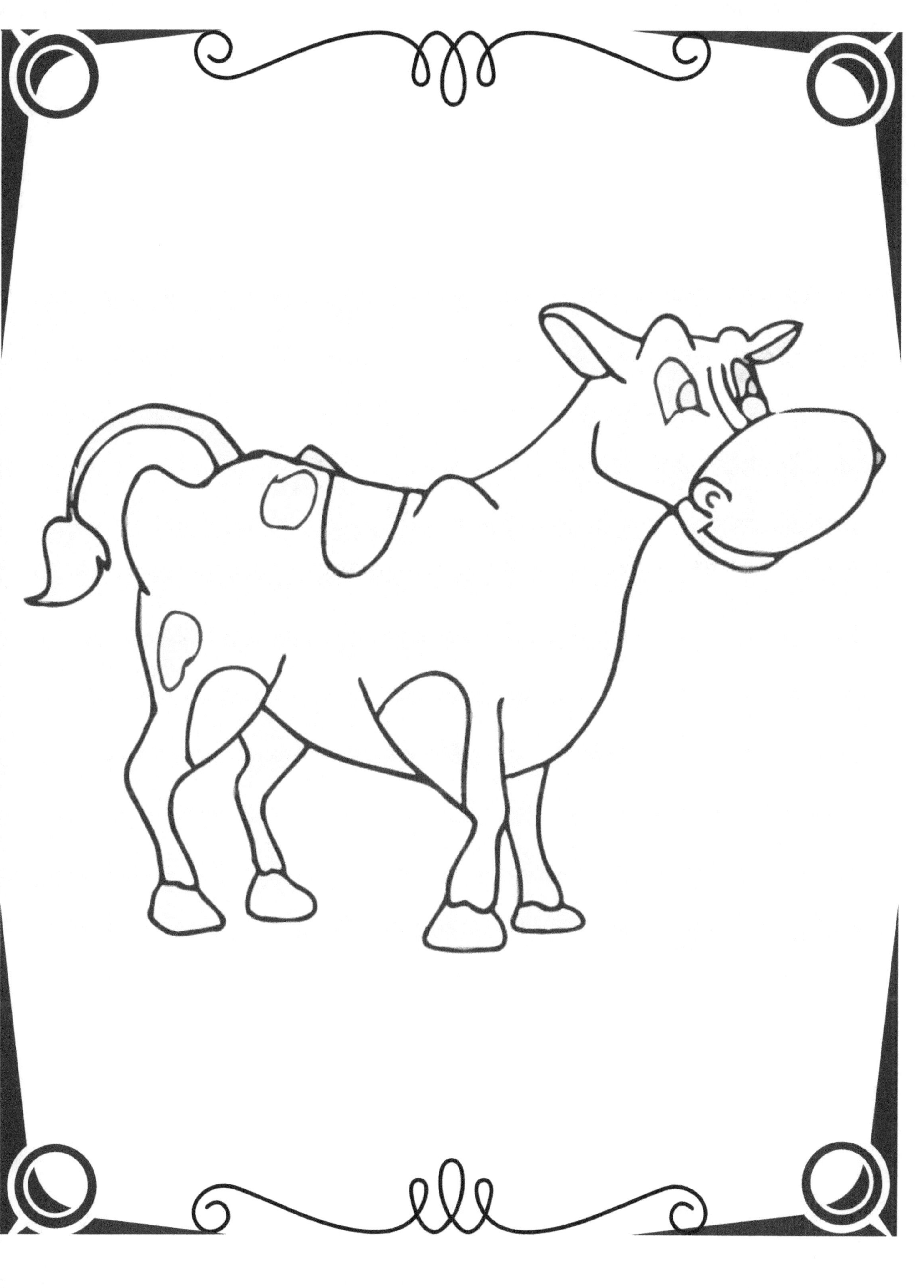

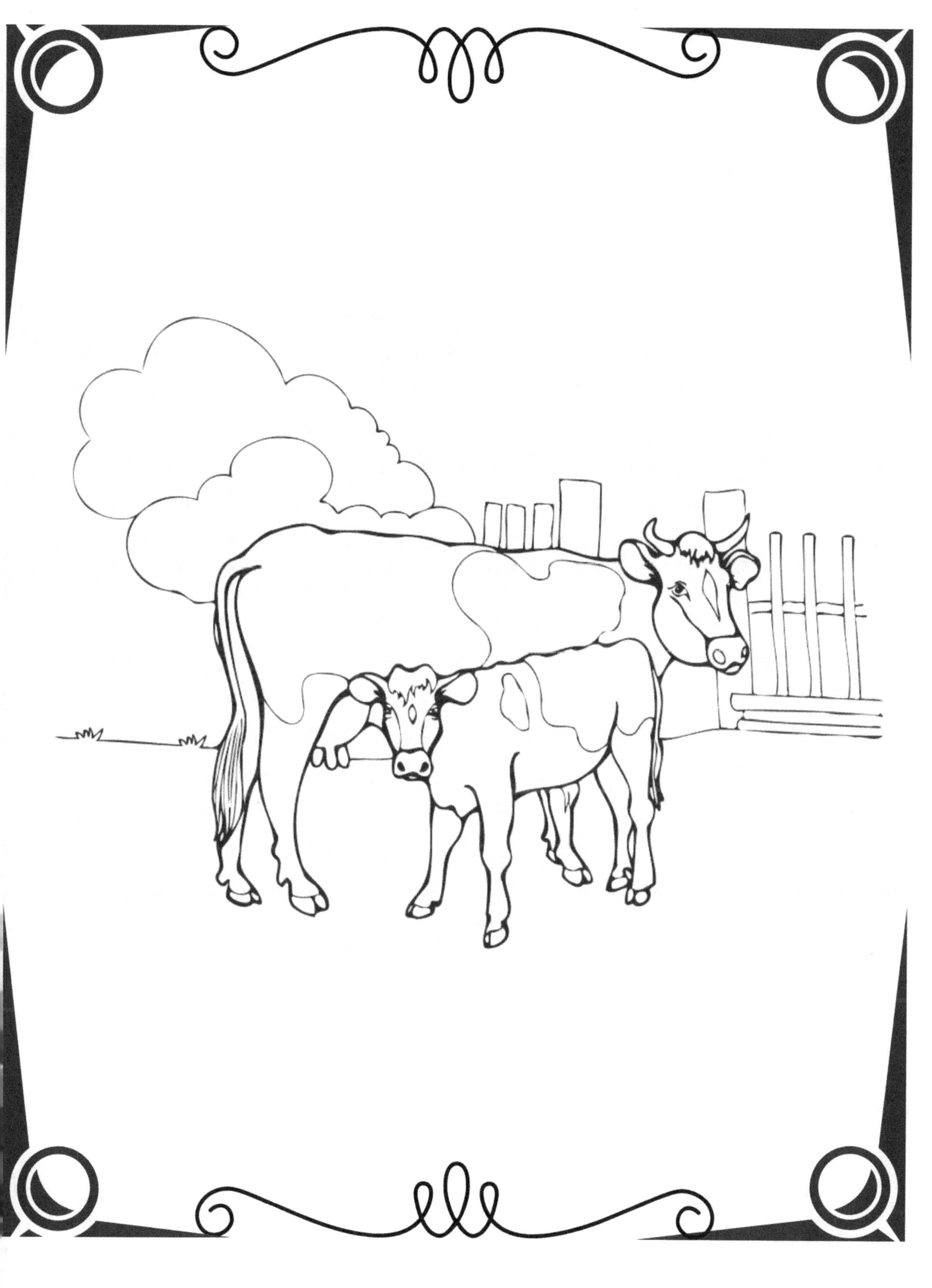

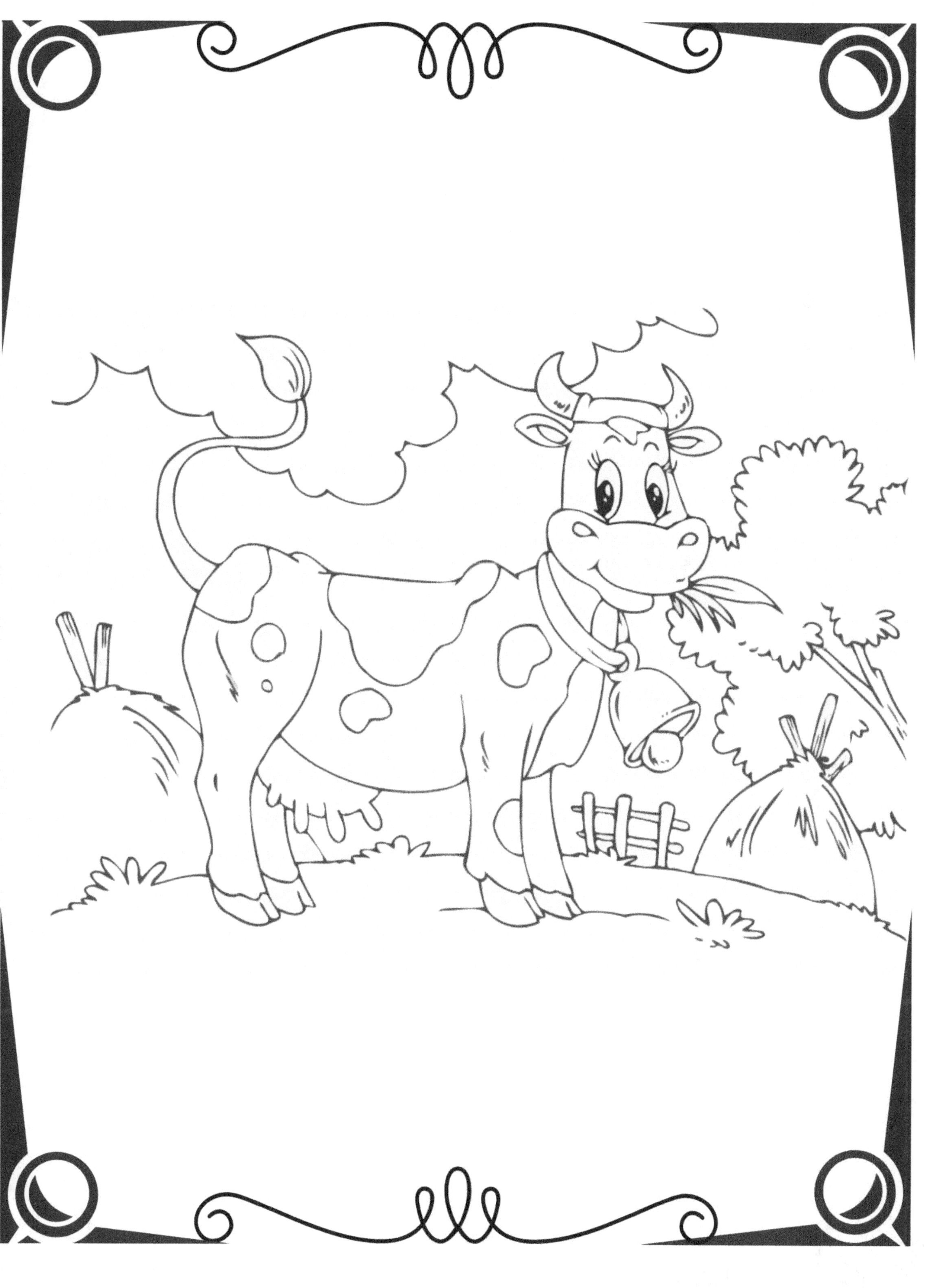